Conceived in Conscience

Conceived in Crisis

Conceived in Conscience

Edited by Richard A. Rutyna and John W. Kuehl

Donning Company/Publishers
Norfolk/Virginia Beach

Library of Congress Cataloging in Publication Data

Main entry under title:

Conceived in conscience.

    1. Church and state—United States—History—
Addresses, essays, lectures. 2. United States—Politics
and government—Addresses, essays, lectures. 3. United
States—Church history—Addresses, essays, lectures.
I. Rutyna, Richard A. II. Kuehl, John W.
BR516.C688   322.10973   82-23467
ISBN 0-89865-298-7

Printed in the United States of America

Contents

Contents

Preface

Contemporaries who believe that the genius of American politics has been a lack of dogmatism and the ready acceptance of religious diversity see the present activity of the Christian fundamentalist right-wing as reminiscent of the repression of the McCarthy era of the 1950s. Mainline Christian denominations have also become concerned about the active role in politics which groups such as Moral Majority have recently taken. Proponents of Moral Majority and other groups argue that they are merely exercising their responsibilities as citizens in the republic. As Christians, they are working, they insist, to counter the tide of permissiveness and licentiousness in their society. Their concept of Christian stewardship requires that they strive to elect officials who will help to achieve the better America which they envisage.

Critics of an active role for the church in American politics contend that the church enjoys a protected, privileged tax-exempt status in American society because of an American tradition of separation of church and state. Moreover, concern is expressed about the alleged concentration of political influence in the hands of the ministers. Majority-mandated morality may well result, critics fear, in circumscription of the right of other-minded individuals (whether they are religious or secular) to decide for themselves what is moral and immoral.

Since the election of 1980, political commentators and news analysts have made phrases such as "The Christian Right," "The Born Again Vote," and "Moral Militancy" common in the lexicon of the politically articulate. Newspapers have run headlines such as "TV Commercials Used to Combat Religious Politics," "Moral Majority's Influence Disputed," "Evangelicals Elated After Election," and "God Is Anti-ERA, Falwell Says," to mention but a few. Countless syndicated columns and editorials have attempted to evaluate the meaning of the Christian Right. Clearly the potential influence and impact of a Christian bloc deeply committed to political activism has a significance which is not only timely and a matter of considerable public interest, but it is also an issue of

1

vital importance to the future of American society.

For their part, the Christian political activists place great emphasis upon what they perceive as the general moral decay of American society. A tone of moral urgency pervades the sometimes apocalyptic view of concerned citizens who fear that America is rushing headlong toward Armageddon. In political arenas across the country, Christians are being enjoined, particularly through the medium of the modern electronic ministry, to cast ballots in elections from local referenda to the presidential contest. As the "electronic church" becomes more sophisticated in its use of modern technology, it promises to exert broader influence on the electorate.

Although this book makes no claim to answer completely the question, "What is the role of the church in political affairs?" or to resolve differing views conceived in conscience and defended with conviction, it does hope to shed light in an impartial manner on some of the issues which have generated serious misunderstandings. What were the intentions of the founding fathers who approved the First Amendment to the Constitution? What does history tell us about the role of the church in matters of state? Is the "wall of separation" between church and state really there? Should it be?

The answers to these questions are as complicated as they are fascinating. This volume reflects the thinking of scholars, politicians, and concerned citizens who met at a conference held at Old Dominion University which was co-sponsored by the Virginia Foundation for the Humanities and Public Policy. The book is divided into two sections, the first of which treats the historical and constitutional dimensions of the church-state issue. In the second part, observers present their views of practical applications based upon their legislative and advocacy roles in the realm of politics.

The editors wish to express their gratitude to the Virginia Foundation for the Humanities and Public Policy and to Old Dominion University for helping to make this volume possible. They acknowledge a special debt to Heinz K. Meier, Dean of the School of Arts and Letters of Old Dominion University, whose support of this undertaking has provided encouragement.

Norfolk, Virginia
September 1982

The Editors

John W. Kuehl, Chairman of the History Department at Old Dominion University, specializes in the history of American thought and early national United States history. His research interests have focused on the emergence of national identity during the late eighteenth century.

Richard A. Rutyna is Associate Professor of History at Old Dominion University, where he specializes in teaching the history of colonial and revolutionary America and American Civilization. His research interests focus primarily upon the legal, political, and social institutions of the seventeenth and eighteenth century, and upon American culture in general.

About the Authors

The Rev. Charles V. Bergstrom (D.D., Honoris Causa, Upsala College, New Jersey) is Executive Director of the Office for Governmental Affairs, Lutheran Council in the USA. He earned his M. Div. degree at the present Lutheran School of Theology in Chicago (formerly Augustana Theological Seminary). The Rev. Bergstrom has served in pastorates in Connecticut and Massachusetts, and has served on the staff of the Lutheran Council in the USA since 1977. He is one of the spokesmen of People for the American Way, which was founded by Norman Lear to provide opposition to Moral Majority.

Ruth H. Charity (J.D., Howard University) is currently Vice President of the National Association of Black Women Attorneys. A civil rights and political activist of wide experience, she formerly served on the City Council of Danville, Virginia, and as Democratic National Committeewoman from Virginia. Attorney Charity has served on both the President's Committee on Civil Rights Under Law and the Virginia Advisory Committee to the U.S. Civil Rights Commission. She is a cooperating attorney with the NAACP Legal Defense and Educational Fund, and with the Southern Christian Leadership Conference.

Jeremiah A. Denton, Jr. (L.H.D., Honoris Causa, Spring Hill College, Alabama) is a Republican United States Senator from Alabama. Senator Denton earned an M.A. in international affairs from George Washington University in Washington, D.C. He enjoyed a long and distinguished career in the United States Navy, rising to the rank of rear admiral. He last commanded the Armed Forces Staff College in Norfolk. He has been awarded numerous military honors, including the Navy Cross. Admiral Denton was elected to the United States Senate in 1980. *When Hell Was in Session,* which he co-authored with Ed Brandt, is an autobiographical account of Senator Denton's seven-and-one-half-year imprisonment in a North Vietnam prison camp during the Vietnam War. Following his retirement from the U. S. Navy in

5

1977, Admiral Denton founded the Coalition for Decency. He formerly served as a consultant to the president of the Christian Broadcasting Network, Inc., in Virginia Beach. Senator Denton has been awarded numerous honors, including an honorary Doctor of Humanities from St. Leo's College.

Erling T. Jorstad (Ph.D., University of Wisconsin, History) is Professor of History at St. Olaf College, Northfield, Minnesota. He is the author of a number of books dealing with the Christian Right, religious fundamentalism, morality and politics, and contemporary Christian activism.

David Little (Th.D., Harvard University, Christian Ethics) is Professor of Religion and Sociology at the University of Virginia, Charlottesville. He is the author of several books and numerous articles dealing with such issues as comparative religious ethics, morality and secularization, foreign policy and moral rhetoric, and the influence of Thomas Jefferson's views on the Supreme Court's interpretation of the First Amendment.

Edward E. McAteer is the founder and president of The Religious Roundtable, Inc., which has its headquarters in Arlington, Virginia, and is generally recognized as one of the most active Christian lobbying groups in the nation today. Mr. McAteer attended Memphis State University and Southern Law School. After a long career in sales and marketing, he became national field director for Christian Freedom Foundation in 1976. He has served as national field director of Conservative Caucus, and on the boards of numerous religious organizations. He has chaired three Mid-South Evangelistic Crusades, and served as a delegate to the Congress of World Evangelism in Lausanne, Switzerland, in 1974.

Merrill D. Peterson (Ph.D., Harvard University, American Civilization) is Thomas Jefferson Foundation Professor of History at the University of Virginia, Charlottesville, where he is also currently serving as dean of the faculty. Peterson is one of the nation's foremost Jefferson scholars, and has published works on Jefferson, John Adams, and James Madison.

Richard V. Pierard (Ph.D., University of Iowa, History) is Professor of History at Indiana State University, Terre Haute. He has written on the subject of evangelical Christianity and political conservatism, and has co-authored and co-edited several books dealing with Christianity and contemporary affairs. He is also a frequent contributor to some of the leading journals and periodicals in the field of religious studies and history.

6

The Rev. R. G. Puckett (M.Div., Southern Baptist Theological Seminary) is executive director of Americans United for Separation of Church and State, which has its headquarters in Silver Spring, Maryland. The Rev. Puckett earned his A.B. degree at Western Kentucky University. He has served in pastorates in Kentucky, Ohio, Florida, and Maryland, and has held several offices, including the presidency, and has served on many committees of the Southern Baptist Convention. In addition, the Rev. Puckett has been editor and associate editor of several regional religious publications. He has served as executive director of Americans United for Separation of Church and State since 1979.

Charles E. Rice (J.S.D., New York University Law School) is Professor of Law at the University of Notre Dame Law School, Notre Dame, Indiana. He is the author of several books dealing with the Supreme Court and public prayer, freedom of association, the abortion controversy, and the theory and practice of the secular state. Rice is also the author of many articles and is co-editor of *The American Journal of Jurisprudence.*

Leonard S. Rubenstein (J.D., Harvard University Law School) is president of the American Civil Liberties Union of Virginia. A member of the law firm of Hirschkop and Grad, Mr. Rubenstein deals extensively in civil rights cases and with public interest legislation. He holds B.A. and M.A. degrees in history from Harvard University, as well as an LL.M. from the Georgetown University Law Center. He has published in the *Harvard Civil Rights-Civil Liberties Law Review.*

Frederick Schauer (J.D., Harvard University Law School) is Cutler Professor of Law at the Marshall-Wythe School of Law, College of William and Mary, Williamsburg, Virginia. A specialist in the area of the First Amendment free speech doctrine, Schauer has published reviews and articles on such matters as pornography, community standards, school law, obscenity, and the philosophy of free speech, and has published a monograph on the law of obscenity.

Cal Thomas (B.A., The American University in Washington, D.C., English Literature) is vice president for communications, Moral Majority, Inc., which has its headquarters in Lynchburg, Virginia. Mr. Thomas is a veteran broadcast journalist, having served with NBC News in Washington in a variety of production, editorial, and reportorial roles. He has twenty-one years of experience in broadcasting, including a stint as a television anchorman with the news department of KPRC in Houston. The co-founder of International Media Service, which provides information to Christian radio stations, Mr. Thomas has also published several Christian books.

G. William Whitehurst (Ph.D., West Virginia University, History) is a Republican United States Congressman from the Second District of Virginia. Congressman Whitehurst was formerly a professor of history and dean of students at Old Dominion University, Norfolk, Virginia. He has served in Congress since 1968. A Norfolk native, Congressman Whitehurst formerly served as board chairman of Ghent United Methodist Church.

PART I

HISTORICAL AND CONSTITUTIONAL PERSPECTIVES

Church-State Relations:
A Historical Perspective
by Erling T. Jorstad

In his essay "Church-State Relations: A Historical Perspective," Erling T. Jorstad maintains that the various constitutional, political, and theological dimensions of the church-state issue must be viewed as historically interrelated and interdependent, reflecting both the complexity of the issue itself and of the society at large. He also sees the American church-state tradition as being the product of a "unique blend" of "practical and daily experience" and carefully considered "rationalistic theories of individual and corporate liberty." As the American church-state tradition evolved out of our collective, shared experience, it fostered values very different from those which characterized the European tradition. According to Jorstad, the most important elements in the American tradition are to be found in that set of values, as represented by pluralism, denominationalism, voluntaryism, and activism.

Jorstad maintains that church-state relations are currently in a state of crisis in America. Why that should be so is his chief concern. There is in all that he says, however, a cautious note of optimism which suggests that if the "recipe" is not yet finalized, perhaps that is as it ought to be.

This essay undertakes to examine the early part of our nation's history for precedents and opinions concerning the issue of church-state relations. The essay which follows takes up the issue in the nineteenth century and complements the historical overview. The two essays are not in complete agreement, however, especially concerning the consequences of immigration.

Church-state relations in America, historically considered, are as interdependent, as complex, and as many-sided as American society, including religion in America, is itself. To state the obvious: they are a unique blend of economic, social, moral, political, constitutional, and other ingredients in a recipe which is not yet completed, and hopefully, as I will explain, never will be locked in place once and for all.

Why is it that problems and answers in church-state relations are not more or less permanently settled, decided, or agreed on? Why does it seem that we today have far more church-state questions before the public, the legislatures, and the courts, than ever before in our history? I will try to give some reasons for that.

To do that, let me suggest two other questions. First, what are the major items on the church-state agenda which we find so vexatious, divisive, and unresolved in our day? I do not mean just the cases on the Supreme Court docket—although that is one excellent source—but a more general list. The second question is, why do we have these questions *now*? More precisely, what historical forces, traditions, and sources have helped bring America to its current situation? The answers, partial and brief as they are here, constitute the primary concern of this essay. This is not to say that a historical perspective fully illustrates or explains the current scene. But obviously, church-state relations in the United States are unique in historical annals; no other society has a history in this realm quite like ours. And we would be ill-informed if we did not have some understanding of how we arrived where we are.

This is a very propitious time for such an investigation because the number of national meetings of persons concerned with contemporary church-state relations in the present political atmosphere has increased sharply in recent months, offering further evidence that we are in the midst of a real crisis in church-state relations. Let me cite a few examples. In February 1981, 300 representatives of some 90 percent of all the American religious bodies, including most major and several smaller (numerically) religious groups, met in Washington, D.C., for a three-day conference calling attention to, and seeking solutions for, what they found to be a growing intrusion of all forms of

12

government into church and religious affairs through regulation and court action. Delegates pinpointed some seventeen specific cases of such concern. In April 1981, at the University of Southern California, delegates attended a three-day conference on "Freedom of Religion in America: Historical Roots, Philosophical Concepts and Contemporary Problems." In May 1981, in Washington, D.C., a two-day conference on the topic "Christianity and Politics: Competing Views" attracted a large number of persons. And in September 1981, a conference at Old Dominion University brought together spokespersons from across the religious and political spectrum to discuss "Church-State Relations and Contemporary American Politics" for two days.

One also finds agendas for church-state relations in periodicals such as *Christian Century* and *Christianity Today,* among others. And the Supreme Court continues to surprise and, sometimes, irritate observers with rulings such as that in early April 1981, 8 to 1, stating that a worker who quits his job because of religious beliefs can collect unemployment compensation. In a sentence which I will use as a transition for where I want to go in this essay, Chief Justice Burger said that the courts (the Supreme Court here overruling the Indiana Supreme Court) "should not undertake to dissect religious beliefs." Those beliefs "need not be acceptable, logical, consistent, or comprehensible to others" to be protected by the Constitution, wrote Burger. Commentators noted that Burger's opinion "marked perhaps one of the court's broadest and most emphatic readings of the First Amendment guarantee of religious freedom."

Why? How could that come about? Why are the issues still unsettled, the recipe not complete? And, why are so many persons concerned? The historical record here can yield some clues. My thesis would be this: the tradition of church-state relations is a unique blend of, first, practical and daily experience born out of the necessity for a wide variety of religious bodies to survive in an often hostile physical environment, knowing the enmities of religious conflict brought over from Europe, but determined to establish religious freedom for themselves and their descendants; and, second, the very carefully thought-out, rationalistic theories of individual and corporate liberty enunciated especially by Jefferson and Madison, and later embroidered by certain justices of the Supreme Court. So, we have two sources for our recipe: practical experience—those who wanted religious freedom for themselves discovered they would have to extend it to other groups; and the formal statements which emerged during the Enlightenment and were nurtured during the War for Independence by philosopher-statesmen.

To that, you may say, "So what? Why is this thesis important?" It means—this combination of practical experience and theoretical principle—that church-state relations emerged not by fiat of a king or a council or one denomination; but out of the collective, shared experience of the great majority of Americans who knew from experience that as the First Amendment provides, there should be no established religion and everyone should be free to exercise his own faith, or free to exercise no faith, and be protected in that choice. That, plus Article VI of the Constitution, which prohibits a religious test for office, somehow rang true for most Americans in 1789—not unanimously, because on the state level several restrictions still applied, but rang true in defining what the national government should and should not do. Putting it another way, everyone wanted the national government to stay out of religious matters. For some this was to be as close to total religious freedom as possible; to others, this would be religious toleration of a wide variety of bodies. Freedom and toleration are not quite the same things; but whether freedom or toleration, it was not to be regulated by the national government.

That would be my answer, thus far, to, "So what?" The broader, the deeper, the more widely accepted a practice such as separation of church and state is for a society, the more its citizenry wants to preserve it over the centuries.

I

Now let us turn to the matter of experience and the practical daily solutions keeping the government from dominating the religious lives of the people as was being done in Europe. First, even though several of the original groups of settlers in this nation had no intention of creating any form of disestablishment, or full religious freedom, the economic necessities for survival forced them to employ workers outside their religious traditions who did not take kindly to rigorous regimentation. Second, those proprietors and entrepreneurs with sizeable grants from the Crown wanted the most dependable, responsible workers available for economic development. Frequently these turned out to be groups such as one or more of the several branches of Anabaptists, who were not cooperative with the local prince in, say, a Germanic state, and valued the opportunity to establish their own religious community more highly than they did remaining under what they believed to be an evil or corrupt government. Hence, the bargain was struck: encourage Anabaptists to come here where they could worship as they chose, and in return receive their hard, responsible labor in developing the economic opportunities of the New World. That was very practical.

Most of the leaders of these first colonies were educated not only in the law but also in theology and ethics. To them, no society could long survive if it failed to create a means of enforcing morality by instructing the young in the faith and providing religious auspices for the most solemn, major events of life (birth—baptism—marriage—death). These were understood as religious matters to be dealt with by the churches. In times such as these, the churches held strong power over the lives of the people, whether they be church people or not.

Yet, despite the fact that colonies such as Massachusetts, Virginia, and Connecticut did have constitutional provisions for a religious establishment in their charters, they could not match or overpower their competition—the dissenters who wanted the maximum degree of religious freedom, and not just religious toleration. These included Anne Hutchinson, Roger Williams (though some will dissent on his being a dissenter), the Calverts, the many Baptists, and those untold numbers of converts from the Awakenings who asserted that religious faith was a matter of individual choice and that God spoke and acted directly through the individual rather than through a board of elders. No one before the War of Independence stated in systematic, analytic fashion the philosophical or theological reasons for this, but daily, practical experience dictated and repeated over and again the common sense of preserving one's freedom of religious expression and allowing non-conforming groups the same privilege.

One further point about the colonial ingredients in the recipe. As we read the great documents of the colonial era, we note wide diversity, the recognition of the right to speak freely, and the lack of any centralized ecclesiastical or political agency for approval. All this was different from Europe. Traditions, roots, practices, and legends, a whole shelf full of ingredients for our recipe, are to be found in these documents, based as much as anything on practical experience.

Then came the War for Independence, and a superb opportunity for the citizens to write into their state constitutions precisely what they believed, without having to ask any higher authority for permission. These constitutions give us an insight into our forefathers' values and convictions. We must look closely at their attitudes toward church-state relations because so many of our values and traditions were articulated at this time. In fact, to make this explicit, one of America's major scholars on religious life, Sidney Mead, says:

> The Revolutionary Epoch is the hinge upon which the history of Christianity in America really turns. During this period, forces and tendencies long gathered during the colonial period, culminated in new expressions which came to such dominance that a fresh direction was given to the

thought patterns and institutional life of the churches. The symbolic center of these new expressions is found in the declarations of religious freedom and separation of church and state by that strange coalition of rationalist and pietist.

What evidence have we, however, that the states, now no longer colonies, understood and implemented the separation of church and state? The record is not all that impressive if one follows the strict separationist school (best exemplified today by, say, Leo Pfeffer). In almost every state some constitutional provision was implemented reducing religious freedom. Some states required office-holders to profess publicly their faith in Christianity and the validity of the Testaments. Others, including some of these states, excluded Jews or non-Christians from office-holding. In Georgia and New Hampshire, all legislators had to be Protestant. In New Hampshire, municipalities could promote Protestant teachings of "piety, religion and morality" at their own cost. Massachusetts and Connecticut did much the same. Therefore, while obvious physical persecution toward dissenters did not exist, when the new states had the opportunity to state their beliefs, they generally excluded non-Christians and required pro-Protestant oaths for taking office.

As the states attempted to implement their constitutions, including the church-state provisions, they had considerable trouble. The establishment clauses, the loyalty oaths, and the taxes for sectarian education, seemed contrary to the practical experience and common sense of those citizens who concerned themselves with such matters. They were not able to give articulate expression to their dissent, however, until Thomas Jefferson in the Virginia General Assembly gave expression to the other ingredient in the American church-state recipe—the formal, rational theory.

The statements of Jefferson and Madison in this era were fundamental to the whole question. Jefferson's bill for estab-lishing religious freedom in 1779 said, in part:

Well aware that Almighty God has created the mind free; that all attempts to influence it by temporal punishments or burdens or by civil incapacitations tend only to beget habits of hypocrisy and meanness, and are a departure from the plan of the Holy Author of our religion, who being Lord both of body and mind, yet chose not to propagate it by coercions on either, as was in His Almighty power to do; that the impious presumption of legislators and rulers, civil as well as ecclesiastical, who, being themselves but fallible and uninspired men have assumed domination over the faith of others, setting up their own opinions and modes of thinking as the only true and infallible, and as such endeavoring to impose them on others....

A bill much like this was again attempted in 1784, and this time Madison led the attack. Among the reasons he listed for strict separation, these seem the most relevant: first, religion is exempt from the authority of society. It is a personal concern, secure from a legislative body whose jurisdiction is derivative. Second, any established church is a sign of weakness because it suggests its proponents have a decided lack of faith in their own convictions. Third, history shows that where establishment has existed, so too has pride, indolence, bigotry, and superstition. To be sure, the good order and virtue of a society rest upon law which has divine authority, but such authority can never be coerced.

Then followed the Constitution, the lightning-rod of church-state relations. The Constitution is an amazing document regarding the question of whether this country is "under God." It contains, of course, two clauses or sections relating directly to our concern: Article VI, which says "no religious test shall ever be required as a qualification to any office or public trust under the United States" (that part of the Constitution about which John F. Kennedy needed to remind fellow Americans frequently in 1960) and the First Amendment embracing the disestablishment clause and the free exercise clause. Note that, in contrast to the Declaration of Independence, no invocation is made to God. The one reference to God is in the conclusion—"in the year of our Lord." No session of the convention at Philadelphia in 1787 included prayer, and in the six purposes of the new government enumerated in the Preamble, all were limited to secular matters. So the Constitution adds up to something less than an explicit "Christian" witness or testimony. The assumption was that the federal government would stay out of religious matters because the latter belonged to the states. The federal government opted for religious freedom over religious toleration.

But that did not occur; more accurately, what did happen was that loyalty oaths, tests for office, restrictions against Catholics, Jews, and others, and establishment clauses, gradually faded away in the states. The last vestige of anything like "establishmentism" vanished from the statute books of Massachusetts in the late 1830s.

II

Why did this gradual disappearance of the provisions of the 1770s constitutions take place? To answer that adequately would take volumes, but the answer can be suggested by several key words. Granted they are oversimplifications, but they represent specific, traditional American values. They are—and they will occupy our attention for the balance of this essay—pluralism, denominationalism, voluntaryism, and activism.

Briefly, pluralism, already established by the combination of practical experience and doctrinal insight, was vastly strengthened in the nineteenth century by two forces, immigration on a mammoth scale, and industrialization which helped attract immigrants here. When the number of immigrants from the British Isles and western European countries started to decline, to be replaced by large numbers from southern and eastern Europe, the religious diversity of the population was vastly expanded. By 1914 every country in Europe was represented in America. Virtually every denomination, and every variation of the major and minor religious subgroups from Catholicism, Protestantism, and Orthodoxy, had its representatives on these shores.

What is fascinating about this is that although considerable friction, and sometimes violence in the form of nativism and anti-Catholic, anti-Jewish, and anti-Mormon hostility broke out, the Supreme Court waited until 1878 before making any major decisions on the non-establishment and free exercise clauses. In fact, it ruled then only on the former. Somehow the whole question had been left alone to be settled, apparently, by very vigorous and often nasty local battles over public versus private schools, the teaching of religious subjects in public schools, and a brief but spectacular flurry over regulating polygamy among Mormons and complex marriages among Oneida Perfectionists.

My point? Despite efforts by Protestants to limit the numbers and influence of non-Protestant Christians, America proved in the nineteenth century to be hospitable in many ways to a variety of religious bodies, strengthening the trend toward pluralism as the nation matured.

The second word: denominationalism. As Mead shows so well, it is a uniquely American institution, made possible by America's separation of church and state. He writes,

It has no official connection with a civil power whatsoever. A church as a church has no legal existence in the United States. It is represented legally by a civil corporation in whose name the property is held and the necessary business transacted. Neither is the denomination a sect in a traditional sense and certainly not in the most common sense of a dissenting body in relationship to an established church. It is, rather, a voluntary association of like-hearted and like-minded individuals who are united on the basis of common beliefs for the purpose of accomplishing tangible and defined objectives.

Note the emphasis upon freedom over toleration.

Given what we have established so far, what occurred largely in the nineteenth century was the full-flowering of the voluntary denomination, the formal expression of pluralism. Using both their understanding of religious freedom and the geographical frontier, Americans utilized that freedom to remove any traditional civil and ecclesiastical restrictions on the expression of the religious convictions of the populace. The frontier provided the necessary opportunities and space in which such expressions could survive.

Crucial to all this is our third word, voluntaryism, or the voluntary principle, the necessary corollary of religious freedom. These free religious groups became voluntary associations equal before, but independent of, the civil power and each other. Accepting religious freedom, they in essence surrendered coercive power, depending upon persuasion alone. This has had enormous ramifications, right up to the present day. As a voluntary association, the church places its primary emphasis on the free, uncoerced consent of the individual. Having already won religious freedom, the voluntary denomination was free to define its own particular objectives.

Let us now move to a brief summary of the specific implications for American religious life that pluralism, denominationalism, and voluntaryism have. I rely here largely upon the recent study by Catherine Albanese, *America: Religion and Religions*. She suggests that out of this blend just mentioned comes a pattern of activism: "denominationalism and voluntaryism meant that individuals had to take part in energetic efforts to advance the cause for their religion among their fellow citizens." Note that it is the individuals who do this, the voluntary groups, and not any governmental agency.

From this comes "a religious outlook, a spiritual style that put its premium on public behavior" in contrast to the privatized churches of, say, western Europe or Russia. Albanese goes on to make a point for our consideration. Given all this voluntaryism, denominationalism, pluralism, religious freedom, and activism, she says, "Protestant activism in the end melted into the larger activism of the American culture, for Protestantism was indeed public." This activist impulse, she argues, led to "reductionism." That means reducing things to their lowest common denominator, their simplest terms. This stems from activism because the latter stimulated a cutting-away of religion to the bare essentials. To build a Protestant civilization, Americans did not have much time for niceties and elaborations, whether of religion or anything else. This led to moral crusades as the common denominator—quick fix, instant solutions for dancing, card playing, prohibition—all coming out of personal piety. Albanese shows this trend continuing up to our day.

Many Americans, Protestant and Catholic, are reductionists in their moral outlook. For instance, Albanese writes, "sex outside of marriage was wrong and Christian witness was right. Gambling and alcohol led to trouble, but love for country and loyalty in war were right and good." Out of this comes what I have called in another place, "moralism." That is the teaching nurtured in the nineteenth century, and flowering again in full-bloom in our day, that for every moral decision to be made, God has given us the one, single, only correct moral course of action to follow. We know what this course of action is because it resides in the inerrant, infallible, inspired Bible.

III

It is the public nature of Protestantism that is important for our consideration here. Protestantism did not remain inward, purely spiritualistic, or reflective. It took a practical, public turn. Churches decided they had the responsibility and freedom to influence the public behavior of those outside their own group discipline as well as that of their own members. The nation, so the argument went, rested on maintaining firm, absolute moral principles. Without these, Americans would sink into the decay so evident in the godless nations of Europe.

What I am suggesting is that church-state relations have remained in a state of evolving, or becoming; the recipe is not yet fixed. That is a most remarkable result of the vision of Jefferson and Madison. A vocal number of Americans today are finding different ways, apart from the mainstream, to apply practicality, rationality, voluntaryism, denominationalism, activism, and religious freedom (rather than religious toleration) to public issues.

Yet the question remains to be addressed, "Why, if so few major church-state cases have come before the courts earlier, is there such a flood of them now?" "Why is there a major conflict upon which so much depends, or upon which the stakes for so many people are high?"

The stakes *are* very high today. Why? In part because the argument has been made that unless America undergoes a drastic turnaround in its moral behavior, both personal and social, the nation will collapse into oblivion and decay.

What has happened is that a decision has been made by a considerable, well-organized, well-financed portion of the American electorate to use the power of the national government—not the Supreme Court, but the legislature and, if possible, the executive—to enforce a specific code of morality on a religiously and moralistically pluralistic society.

Radicalism of the Right
and Religious Freedom
by Richard V. Pierard

Richard V. Pierard, whose essay "Radicalism of the Right and Religious Freedom" is presented here, maintains that "the close ties that have existed between right-wing extremist movements and religion are a prominent feature of American history." In developing this thesis, Pierard surveys some of the notable examples of rightist tendencies which have been manifested by Protestant and Roman Catholic adherents alike from the nineteenth century to the modern era. After discussing the relationship between religion and such forces as "nativism" and "Americanism," Pierard concludes that "the record of right-wing radicalism in protecting and enhancing religious freedom in the United States is not a good one."

The focus of this essay is upon the divisiveness and intolerance which the author sees as the result of combining religion with right-wing politics. He is not optimistic as to the future prospect of the political right advancing the cause of religious freedom, and he draws a distinction between "moral" issues and issues which he characterizes as "religious" in nature, while suggesting that the radical right-wing confuses the two.

21

The close ties that have existed between right-wing extremist movements and religion are a prominent feature of American history. The literature detailing that fact is indeed vast. My intention here is to review that connection and to demonstrate that, in spite of all their affirmations of Christian concern and devotion to the church, the representatives of the far right throughout our history have both in their actions and words manifested a tendency to abridge and constrict the religious freedom that is enshrined in the Bill of Rights and which is a hallmark of American life. This is a matter of particular interest to me because I come out of a conservative evangelical tradition that is much concerned about preserving its own right to religious liberty. That tradition is also one, however, whose spokesmen have all too often identified with groups whose political goals seemed attractive but whose endeavors inexorably led in the direction of restricting the very freedom they so deeply prized.

I

The linkage of religion and political extremism was established early in the history of the republic. For example, the Anti-Masonic movement of the late 1820s and 1830s portrayed the Freemasons as a conspiratorial order of evil and immoral men who were seeking to gain control of politics and community life and who had to be headed off by whatever means necessary. Evangelicals saw the necessity to defend their faith against "the last great effort on the part of the forces of darkness to destroy religion," and portrayed Masonry as an "infidel society" at war with true Christianity. Before long the liberal religions, Unitarianism and Universalism, were brought into the plot together with Catholics and Jews, and "Masonry and Catholicism, dread oaths, and the Inquisition became linked in the minds of the people," according to R. A. Billington.

Conspiracy theories held a particular attraction for evangelicals, and almost invariably they were drawn to these rightist groups that saw things in conspiratorial terms. That the underlying issues feeding Anti-Masonry were actually political and social in nature no one will deny, but the precedent of joining religion and right-wing radicalism had been established.

Nativist extremist groups soon appeared on the scene that

expressed through a virulent anti-Catholicism a burning sense of resentment over the rising numbers of Irish and German immigrants who thronged into the urban centers, lived in slum areas, dominated the welfare rolls and crime statistics, and competed with the existing working class for jobs. The volume of Catholic immigration threatened what evangelicals perceived as their way of life, and they concluded that a sinister plot was being hatched by the hated "Papists" and their shock troops, the Jesuits. Beginning with the mob action that leveled the Ursuline convent in Charlestown, Massachusetts, in 1834, the slogan "No Popery" took on increasing political as well as religious significance, and eventually parties were formed, the American Republicans in the 1840s and the American party (better known as the Know-Nothings) in the 1850s. Again it was primarily social strains produced by unrestricted immigration that lay behind these movements, but anti-Catholic bigotry was its main stock-in-trade. The principle of religious freedom may have been enunciated in the Constitution, but for these extremists it did not extend to people outside the Protestant mainstream.

To be sure, we should be careful not to equate nativism and anti-Catholicism too quickly, as the latter was certainly a reflection of growing national awareness in the United States. Americans viewed the authoritarian organization of the church and its traditional association with monarchical government with considerable suspicion, and they regarded American liberty and European "popery" as irreconcilable. As the right-wing extremist organizations were strongly patriotic in character, anti-Catholicism invariably was part of their program. This continued to be the case in the years between the Civil War and World War I, and especially so with the American Protective Association.

Founded in 1887, the APA was a secret society, much like the various lodges of the era, with oaths, rituals, and costumes. To belong to it one declared, in the words of the 1894 statement of principles, "loyalty to true Americanism" and expressed the belief that "subjection to and support of any ecclesiastical power, not created and controlled by American citizens, and which claims equal, if not greater, sovereignty than the government of the United States, is irreconcilable with American citizenship." The initiate agreed to uphold the Constitution and its affirmation of religious liberty, but, as D. L. Kinzer explains, with the reservation that this freedom was "guaranteed to the individual" and did not mean "that under its protection any un-American ecclesiastical power can claim absolute control over the education of the children growing up under the Stars and Stripes." Each member solemnly swore not to employ a Catholic when a Protestant was available, not to vote for one, and not to go on strike with one. In his oath he also made the following affirmation:

> I hereby denounce Roman Catholicism. I hereby denounce the Pope, sitting at Rome or elsewhere. I denounce his priests and emissaries, and the diabolical work of the Roman Catholic church, and hereby pledge myself to the cause of Protestantism to the end that there may be no interference with the discharge of the duties of citizenship.

A politically-minded group from the outset, the APA sought to mobilize the working-class vote for Republican candidates in state and local elections, and in 1894 scored some impressive victories. In 1894-1895, it reached a high point of about 2.5 million adherents, but it declined rapidly thereafter when its program was largely co-opted and its leaders thoroughly ignored by the Republicans.

Anti-Semitism began to appear in extremist circles as the influx of immigrants from eastern Europe brought a rapid increase in the number of Jews. There was an element of this in the Populist movement, and its most important Southern leader, Tom Watson, was a virulent anti-Semite. Bigotry was exacerbated when the struggle over U.S. entry into World War I pitted the three most visible immigrant groups—the Irish, Germans, and Jews, all of whom were either anti-British or anti-Tsarist—against the native majority of Anglo-Saxon ancestry. Then, radical nativism and xenophobia was stirred to a fever pitch in the post-war "Red scare," and what resulted was a wave of legislation restricting civil liberties and mass deportations of allegedly subversive aliens. Prohibition and its attendant lawlessness provided the occasion for further anti-foreignism. Finally the torrent of immigrants was reduced to a trickle by the passage of immigration acts in 1921 and 1924 which contained discriminatory national origins quotas, while a new wave of enthusiastic nationalism as well as anti-Catholic and anti-Jewish fervor swept over the land.

In the letdown period after the war, the new extremism portrayed all of the nation's troubles as produced by the cunning of alien influences combined with a lack of sufficient commitment by Americans to resist the forces of darkness. As John Higham aptly puts it: "The evil was too great, the world too deeply infected. Americans must concentrate on holding their present ground." The stage was now set for the resurgence of the Ku Klux Klan.

II

Religious and racial bigotry was elevated to a new level by the Ku Klux Klan. Born in the restless days of Reconstruction, it functioned for a time as a secret vigilante organization, but by 1872 it had passed from the scene. It remained a hallowed memory in the folklore of the South, and national interest in it was rekindled by Thomas Dixon's maudlin novel *The Clansman* (1905) and D. W. Griffith's epic film *The Birth of a Nation* (1915). In the latter year, William J. Simmons revived the organization, and after World War I, it grew into a nationwide movement, with millions of adherents, which emphasized fraternalism and the protection of traditional values. Although the specific objectives of local groups varied widely, they tended to be highly moralistic—upholding the integrity of the family, combating miscegenation, chastising criminals, rooting out bootleggers—primarily those things which appealed to small-town people, many of whom now resided in large cities and were trying to preserve the values of their rural upbringing in an urban environment. As part of its commitment to a native white Protestant nation, the Klan also promoted patriotism, usually labeled as "100% Americanism."

In many parts of the country the "Invisible Empire" blossomed into a formidable political force, even to the point of intimidating state and local governments, electing candidates to office (including a U.S. senator), and turning out hundreds or even thousands of robed marchers in mass demonstrations. In 1924 the Klan played a prominent role in the deliberations of the Democratic National Convention and assisted in Coolidge's election, and in the following year it flexed its muscles in a mammoth Washington march. Before the end of the decade, however, its power had begun to recede rapidly due to its excessive violence and brutality, increasing factionalism and infighting, outright corruption among its leaders, and an essentially negative program that defended against evils which were more imaginary than real.

Particularly noteworthy was the religious bigotry of the Klan. Although it manifested an ongoing aversion to Negroes and Jews, it in fact spent far more time promoting anti-Catholicism than in trying to keep blacks "in their places." David Chalmers' description of the Klan's pattern of operation in Oregon would apply equally well to many other parts of the country:

> First, under the auspices of some Protestant church, an 'escaped nun' would tell of her ordeal. Next, the Klan's anti-Catholic and patriotic pamphlets would be slipped into cars and under doors. Then, a fire-branding evangelist or Klan lecturer would whip up feeling against 'the Roman Octopus which has taken over control in the nation's capital.' Finally, with a local pastor or two leading the way, the Klan would recruit its legions.

In Oregon, the group demonstrated its clout by obtaining passage in 1922 of an initiative, aimed primarily at Roman Catholics, which made public education compulsory for all children; but three years later it was struck down by the Supreme Court (*Pierce v. Society of Sisters*, 1925). The decision was based on the Fourteenth Amendment due process clause and the right of parents to determine the appropriate mental and moral training their children should receive rather than on the guarantee of religious freedom specified in the First Amendment. Commentators still regard it as a landmark ruling in church-state relations. In Ohio, the Klan tried unsuccessfully to push bills through the state legislature requiring public schooling and barring Catholic teachers. One bill stipulating daily Bible reading did pass, but the governor vetoed it on the grounds that it violated the separation of church and state.

The Klan reveled in rumors of Catholic conspiracies. For example, it promoted the spurious Knights of Columbus oath which alleged that members of the fraternal society promised to "hang, burn, waste, boil, flay, strangle, and bury alive" all "heretics, Protestants, and Masons." (It had been exposed as a fake oath by a Congressional committee in 1913.) There was also the whispered story that every time a boy was born to a Roman Catholic family, the father added a rifle and ammunition to the arsenal in his parish church, the accusation that the Pope had purchased the high ground overlooking Washington and West Point, and the hysteria that gripped the simple folk of North Manchester, Indiana, when word got around that the Pope was coming in on the next train from Chicago. Then in 1928 one of the Klan's worst fears came to pass when a Catholic, Alfred E. Smith, was nominated for the Presidency. The nativism and anti-Catholicism which the group helped to foment contributed something to the Hoover landslide, although this was hardly a decisive factor.

To be sure, the Klan's opposition to Catholicism was not so much grounded in theology as in a fear that hierarchical control from Rome prevented Catholics from being fully assimilated into American society. Yet, this feeling certainly contained theological overtones, and the organization drew heavily for its membership upon the more conservative denominations, especially the Baptists, Methodists, and Disciples of Christ. Among the major denominations, the church authorities, conventions, and periodicals almost universally refrained from endorsing the Klan, but many ordinary clerics did succumb to its attraction or were pressured by parishioners and local people to follow the Klan line or at least keep silent. My own grandfather, who served a Presbyterian church in Evansville, Indiana, in the mid-1920s, was threatened by the local Klan chapter for befriending

Catholics.

David Chalmers points out, correctly I believe, that the real lure of the Klan was that it "appeared to be doing what the Church talked about. It promised to bring Christian righteousness to society, to make it dry and moral." In short, it would "make the community as it ought to be." That to achieve such a noble objective required that one ride roughshod over American freedoms did not seem to bother this "Moral Majority" of the 1920s.

III

With the onset of the Depression, the Klan was eclipsed by even more excessive forms of right-wing extremism. These individuals and groups generally emphasized class and interest politics more than simply affirming the moral virtues of the past, and they usually offered some sort of program for the future. The old-fashioned nativism was replaced by a highly charged nationalism ("Americanism") and an abstract kind of racism directed especially at Jews, although of course Negroes were not ignored. The anti-Semitism they expressed was as much racial in nature as religious. Finally, for many on the right the experiments of Mussolini's Italy and Hitler's Germany held peculiar fascination. Two noteworthy religious personalities who represented the new trends on the right were the Protestant fundamentalist Gerald Winrod and the Roman Catholic radio preacher Father Charles E. Coughlin.

A self-educated evangelist from Kansas, Winrod set out in the 1920s to save America from "godless liberalism." Never the holder of a pastorate nor identified with a specific Protestant denomination, he engaged in itinerant preaching and journalism. In 1926, he founded the *Defender Magazine* which ten years later had a circulation of 100,000. Like most fundamentalists of the period, he and his organization, the Defenders of the Christian Faith, concentrated on denouncing Catholics and liberal Protestants ("modernists"), but in the following decade he focused increasingly upon Jews. Winrod publicized the notorious *Protocols of the Elders of Zion,* portrayed contemporary communism as a direct offshoot of a Jesuit-Jewish conspiracy, and suggested that the ecumenical modernists held Jewish views and were essentially not only judaized Protestants but also fronts for Jewish communism. After visiting Germany in 1934, he became an apologist for the National Socialist regime, even to the point of saying that the unpleasantness Jews were experiencing there was not nearly as bad as the "Jewish-inspired" persecution of Russian Christians after the Bolshevik Revolution. In 1938, the Kansas preacher decided to make the U.S. Senate a sounding board for his bigoted ideas and ran on a platform of "Let's keep Christian

America Christian—let's keep America safe for Americans," but he was soundly trounced in the Republican primary.

Because Winrod had such close connections with mainline American evangelical Protestants, his racism, super-patriotism, and anti-democratic views could not help but have a negative influence on them and reinforce already deeply-held prejudices. For instance, William B. Riley, one of the leading fundamentalists, believed in the validity of the *Protocols* and worked closely with Winrod in promoting racism—both white supremacy and anti-Semitism—among Protestant clergymen. Although he may have had the greatest impact in evangelical circles, others as well sowed the seeds of anti-Semitic hate among theological conservatives, including Gerald L. K. Smith, Harvey Springer, and William Dudley Pelley.

Winrod also used his position as the head of a religious movement to attempt to influence political events. During the 1936 election campaign, starting with President Roosevelt and going down the line, he publicly lumped the leading members of the administration in the category of Jews and labeled proponents of Social Security and other New Deal legislation as being in league with "international Jewry that is seeking to dominate the Christian world." In the following year, the Kansas fundamentalist maintained that he was doing God's work as he mounted a campaign of opposition to Roosevelt's scheme to reorganize the Supreme Court. According to Gustavus Myers, he dispatched letters to all members of Congress declaring his stance and flatly stating that his magazine had "the largest and most select group of Protestant readers in the United States....There are indications that God had brought us together for just such a specific work at this particular time." When a senator accused him of unfairly trying to influence legislators and distorting public opinion, Winrod retorted with the boast that he could have at least 15,000 pastors of all denominations "take the fight into the pulpit Sunday if I think it necessary." The Klan had used similar pressure tactics, and religiously oriented right-wing groups would repeatedly do likewise in the ensuing decades.

An even more remarkable endeavor was that of Father Coughlin, a Canadian-born priest of Irish-American extraction who was assigned to a parish in Detroit in 1923. Three years later he began broadcasting over the radio, mainly on religious matters, and used this means to raise funds to build his church in suburban Royal Oak which was to be a shrine to St. Theresa of the Little Flower, a recently canonized French nun. In 1930, he went on a national network and started speaking on political and economic topics as well. Before long he was inundated with mail from Catholics and Protestants alike, the volume of which ran around 80,000 letters per week while a sermon on Hoover's economic policy drew 1.2 million responses. By 1939, his weekly audience was computed by the Institute of Public Opinion to be 3.5 million, and his magazine *Social Justice* claimed a circulation of one million. As the money flowed in, Coughlin was able to complete his $750,000 church and employ a team of reseachers to gather information for his discourses and a huge clerical staff to handle the correspondence. He did no parish work himself, and in many ways his activities foreshadowed those of the electronic church which emerged in the 1970s.

His early addresses contained a distinct anti-communist flavor but also came down heavily on the behavior of American capitalists and particularly the banking interests. To help promote his idea of a vague "state capitalism," Coughlin formed the National Union for Social Justice. Although originally a supporter of Roosevelt, he broke with the New Deal and in 1936 jumped into the political arena by endorsing Congressional candidates and the third party presidential hopes of William Lemke whose program was similar to Coughlin's. After Lemke's poor showing, the radio priest adopted an increasingly more aggressive and fascist-like stance. He attacked American politicians for being soft on communism, denounced democracy, called for the abolition of political parties, and advanced a corporate state proposal whereby congressmen would be elected by functional or occupational groups rather than in districts.

As the decade advanced, Coughlin's pronouncements became anti-Semitic as well as pro-fascist. In 1937, he began attacking Jews as communists and formed so-called Social Justice Councils from which all "non-Christians" were excluded. The following year he created the Christian Front which was intended to force industrial capitalism to yield a fair share of its wealth to labor and to "curb the Molochs of international finance." He said the Christian Front would "not fear to be called 'anti-Semitic'" nor would it be "afraid of the word 'fascist.'" He made copious use of the *Protocols of the Elders of Zion* in an endeavor to prove that tyranny, oppression, and poverty were the result of Jewish machinations to control the world's wealth and promote revolutionary doctrines. He defended Nazi persecution of the Jews, attacked moves to aid the Allies in Europe in 1940-1941, and blamed the war, and efforts to draw the United States into it, on the Jews. To avoid the embarrassment of a sedition trial, Coughlin's superior finally and permanently silenced him in May 1942.

The movement did much to poison Jewish-Christian relations, and it clearly offered proletarian fascism as a substitute for American democracy. Basically, however, the right-wing Americanism of the Coughlinites offered protection not against aliens as such but against people with alien ideas. The Detroit priest merged nativism and conspiracy into a single focus, and the abstract Jew embodied the abstract alien in the nation's midst. This lay beneath his action in advancing the theory of an international Jewish conspiracy of bankers and communists. The conspiratorial Jew was the "International Banker" who retarded the growth of power and status among the lower class. In contrast to what normally had been the populist and left-wing image, Coughlin transformed the abstract Jew into the alien communist who leveled all statuses and values, and suggested the new demon had to be resisted by all means possible.

IV

In the post-war years, the focus of the far right shifted to communism, although there were still substantial pockets of anti-Negro and anti-Jewish hatred. To be sure, communism had been in the purview of the right since the Russian Revolution, but it became an all-encompassing obsession only after 1945. Roman Catholics were drawn to this cause early; in the late 1930s some had discovered anti-communism as a means whereby they could identify with the greater American society. As David O'Brien puts it: "In fighting the red peril the Catholic could dedicate himself to action which was both Catholic and American. Few would disagree that he was proving his worth as an American and demonstrating the compatibility of faith and patriotism." He was showing that the church "was a necessary ally and valuable asset to America, the strongest supporter of her ideals and institutions."

Anti-communism thus could function as the bulwark of both true Americanism and authentic Catholicism. Much of this emotional feeling was directed toward the plight of the church in eastern Europe, but some Catholics gravitated toward the far right and formed small anti-communist groups similar to those found among Protestant extremists. The most noteworthy of these were the Cardinal Mindszenty Foundation, an "educational" organization headquartered in St. Louis that informed Catholics about the dangers of communism, and the Manion Forum, a radio broadcast and newsletter in which the former dean of the University of Notre Dame Law School (now deceased) exposed the evils of communism, liberalism, and pacifism. Some prominent clerics were outspoken foes of communism, above all Francis Cardinal Spellman and Bishop Fulton J. Sheen, and associations like the Catholic War Veterans and Knights of Columbus actively promoted anti-communism. But when it came to Senator Joseph McCarthy, himself a Catholic, churchmen were more ambivalent. Conservatives responded positively to his call to arms in the struggle between "our Western Christian world and the atheistic Communist world" while liberals were strongly critical of McCarthyism. As a result the Catholic community in general was not favorably inclined towards demands for a thoroughgoing Red-hunt.

It is fair to say that Catholic concern about communism was congruent with official and public attitudes of the late 1940s and the 1950s. They shared the feeling that all Americans were required to do battle for the Lord in the apocalyptic struggle between freedom and tyranny. As Father Donald Crosby points out: "In such a climate compromise became equated with appeasement and dissent with heresy."

While Catholics were able to keep their extreme right under a modicum of restraint, even though they adopted an unshrinking anti-communist stance, the issue was far more divisive in Protestant ranks. There a number of militant groups used the question to foster schism in churches, discredit progressive leaders, and throttle expression of dissent. Already in the 1930s the Federal Council of Churches had been condemned for allegedly promoting socialism, communism, internationalism, and pacifism in such inflammatory works as E. N. Sanctuary's *Tainted Contacts* (1931) and Elizabeth Dilling's *The Red Network* (1934), and this was accentuated in the post-war volume by John T. Flynn, *The Road Ahead* (1949), which charged that "a clique of Christian ministers and laymen" were "using" the Federal Council "to promote the interests of a Socialist revolution in America." Presbyterian fundamentalist Carl T. McIntire created the American Council of Christian Churches in 1941 to counter the influence of ecumenical organizations, and he repeatedly expressed the conviction that the crises facing America, especially communism, could be traced to "apostasy" in its churches. Regarding the World Council of Churches, McIntire wrote in 1949 that it had become "an ally with Russia in the struggle to undermine the capitalistic West. They are united in that purpose." Before long, a bevy of other rightists mounted attacks on "mainline" Protestant denominational figures and agencies. The best-known among these critics included Edgar C. Bundy, Verne P. Kaub, Billy James Hargis, and Myers G. Lowman.

The unrelenting rightist assault on liberal churchmen eventually attracted the attention of the communist witch-hunters in Washington. In March 1953, Representative Harold H. Velde suggested that the House Committee on Un-American Activities (HUAC) which he chaired might investigate the situation in the churches, and the McIntire faction was jubilant. Methodist Bishop G. Bromley Oxnam was singled out for special treatment but no substantive evidence could be mustered at the hearing in July to prove he was a subversive. Then J. B. Matthews, a former HUAC investigator and ex-leftist, shocked the nation with the assertion in the July 1953 issue of the *American Mercury* that:

The largest single group supporting the Communist apparatus in the United States today is composed of Protestant clergymen....The Communist party has enlisted the support of at least seven thousand Protestant clergymen (as) party members, fellow-travelers, espionage agents, party-line adherents, and unwitting dupes.

Matthews had just been appointed executive director of Senator McCarthy's investigating committee, but the ensuing uproar from the article forced him to resign. Some top clergymen complained directly to President Eisenhower about the allegations, and he publicly endorsed their criticisms.

After McCarthy's fall in 1954, the Protestant far-rightists were disappointed, but they continued their drumfire attacks on liberals in the churches. Many of them utilized existing pressure groups or created new ones such as the Christian Crusade, Church League of America, American Council of Christian Laymen, Circuit Riders, National Education Program, Christian Freedom Foundation, and Christian Anti-Communism Crusade. The Christian rightist organizations together with secular bodies like the John Birch Society and Americans for Constitutional Action eventually became multi-million-dollar operations as a result of the passions stirred by John F. Kennedy's election. They saw in the New Frontier everything they were against, and they did what they could to discredit liberal trends, and some would say, to inject venom into the nation's bloodstream. Examples of what I would regard as their negative influence are: the Air Force training manual scandal of 1960 (its author used material from Hargis that alleged pro-communist tendencies in the National Council of Churches); the bigoted campaign against Kennedy because he was a Catholic; the glorification of the dismissed General Edwin Walker who had used Birch Society items in a citizenship education program for his troops; branding both the Kennedy assassination and the civil rights movement as communist conspiracies; continual carping at the Supreme Court for its ruling on religious exercises in public schools, racial desegregation, and rights of criminal defendants and supposed subversives; and, finally, helping to steamroller the Goldwater nomination in 1964.

It seems clear that during the 1950s and 1960s, Roman Catholics were better able to rein in the exuberance of their right wing than Protestants were. This was probably due to the church's traditional minority status and even more so to the hierarchical principle which made possible a substantial measure of church discipline. As they moved increasingly toward the American mainstream, their commitment to religious liberty strengthened. The Protestant right, on the other hand, continued to be a disruptive force. Their spokesmen rejected the concept of a religious pluralism that would mean full freedom for all faiths and the removal of the state from an active role either in promoting or restraining religious expression among its citizens. They held to the traditional idea of a Christian America (disguised in the innocent phrase "one nation under God") and saw the country as duty-bound to combat atheistic ideologies. Also, the Protestant radical rightists, many of whom gloried in their independence from any kind of church structure or responsibility, pitted Christians against each other and elevated their own political and economic philosophies to the status of religious dogma. Those who did not agree with their views were vilified and regarded either as lower quality Christians or outright unbelievers. After all, there could be no compromise between good and evil. Those dedicated to God and country must defeat anti-Christ communism and its liberal and socialist fellow-travelers if America was to survive.

V

The record of right-wing radicalism in protecting and enhancing religious freedom in the United States is not a good one. Nativists and Klansmen alike manifested little inclination to extend religious liberty to newly-arrived Roman Catholic immigrants or their descendants. Jews were the victims of bigoted propaganda, scapegoating, and outright discrimination. "Americanism" was narrowly defined, virtually in a Protestant evangelical sense, almost up to World War II, when such exclusivity passed out of vogue. Anti-communist witch-hunting set Christian against Christian, and those of more liberal persuasion had their patriotism, as well as theology, called into question.

Looking at the historical evolution of the right, one may justifiably be pessimistic about the commitment of the latest manifestation of this ancient tradition, the "New Right," to preserving religious liberty. Many of their "moral" issues are patently religious in nature—school prayer and abortion, in particular—and their campaign to counter the effects of that vague bogey "humanism" has the earmarks of a crusade. It is strangely inconsistent for preachers who apotheosize separation of church and state to secure through legislation the implementation of programs that are ostensibly moral in nature but at their heart are religious.

Can the "New Right" really affirm religious freedom in the context of American pluralism? Given the historical record, it is doubtful.

Jefferson, Madison, and Church-State Separation
by Merrill D. Peterson

In his essay, "Jefferson, Madison, and Church-State Separa-
tion," Merrill D. Peterson performs a dual role. First, he provides
an incisive commentary on the essays presented here by Profes-
sors Jorstad and Pierard. Second, drawing on his expertise as one
of the nation's foremost Jefferson scholars, he elucidates the
Jeffersonian-Madisonian contribution to the American tradition
of church-state separation.

His commentary on Pierard's and Jorstad's essays calls
attention to the fact that historians viewing the same basic set of
facts need not necessarily come to the same conclusions about
them. In this regard, he perhaps sees Jorstad as more optimistic
than Pierard. He also points out that the precedents which
Pierard cites in tracing right-wing religious activity may not be
entirely justified and that, in any event, one may find earlier
precedents of left-wing religious or quasi-religious activity as
well.

Peterson's discussion of Jefferson's and Madison's contribu-
tions to the American tradition of church-state separation is
essential to an understanding of the general topic. His analysis of
the intellectual climate and the positions of the rationalists and
pietists is noteworthy. In discussing the "wall of separation" and
the movement in Virginia some 200 years ago to legislate religious
freedom, Peterson sketches with keen insight the roles played by
Jefferson and Madison. The conclusion he reaches is that religion
flourished rather than faltered following enactment of the Vir-
ginia Statute of Religious Freedom, and religious tyranny (in the
form of a religious establishment) disappeared. Finally, the
author warns that all of us, whether rationalists or evangelicals,
must adhere to our nation's founding principles if liberty is to be
preserved.

It is evident in the essay presented here, though less clearly than in his other published work, that Richard Pierard writes out of deep concern to protect the "conservative evangelical tradition," as he calls it, from right-wing political penetration. Caring about the health of that tradition, which is essentially apolitical, he worries about the right-wing infection and in his essay takes a look at some of its historical antecedents. Reading the essay I could not help but think, contrapuntally, of the opposite set of linkages, that is, of religion and the political left. Pierard notes that Coughlinites and their ilk associated liberal Protestantism with socialism, communism, internationalism, and other "alien ideas"; he seems to regard this as a product of hysteria or deceit or perhaps both. And so it may have been. But were not many liberal churchmen, in fact, associated with liberal and leftist causes politically? Was not the radicalism on the religious right nurtured, to some extent, by fears of the radicalism on the religious left? And if so, is it possible to understand one without an understanding of the other?

Pierard does not reach back into the eighteenth century for evidence or examples. Had he done so—had he reached into the stormy political history of the 1790s, for instance—he would surely have observed the close connection between the pulpit and the conservative political party of that day, the Federalists, especially in New England. Prominent orthodox clergymen feared the religion, or irreligion, as well as the politics of the Jeffersonian Republicans. They denounced the radicalism of that opposition party and went on to tie it into an alleged international conspiracy led by a notorious sect of Freemasons, the Bavarian Illuminati. In the critical presidential election of 1800 they warned that a Republican victory would be followed by the rape of the church together with a fair portion of the maidens of New England. (Curiously, the Scotsman John Robinson's book, *Proofs of a Conspiracy*, in 1798, which broadcast the idea of an Illuminati plot against Christianity, was republished in 1967 under the auspices of the John Birch Society.)

My point is not, God forbid, to lend credibility to those fears, but to recognize that they had some basis in historical reality. There were Freemasonry and the Illuminati, and both were, in fact, linked to the radicalism of the French Revolution. In the eyes of conservatives, the Illuminati were a kind of radical Jesuitry, aspiring to become the priesthood of the revolutionary new order. Not the same, yet similar, was the revolutionary deism of Thomas Paine. As set forth in *The Age of Reason,* it both outraged and terrified Christians of most denominations as well as most Federalists. There was, in short, a secular religion of the left. And fears of a left-wing takeover drove many Christians to the far right.

Interestingly, Pierard begins his paper with the Anti-Masonic movement of the Jacksonian era. This established, he says, "the precedent of joining religion and right-wing radicalism." But surely, as I have suggested, the precedent was already established. Moreover, I think it is misleading to view Anti-Masonry as right-wing. Employing conventional Republican rhetoric, it attacked the Masonic order as an odious aristocracy and was a precursor of the broad movement of democratic reform in the North. Anti-Masonry, it is true, had a large evangelical following. So, in time, would other reform movements, temperance for instance. It was an age when evangelical Christianity, at least in the northern states, was more left than right in its political orientation.

There is a larger question here of whether Anti-Masonry and similar movements ought to be considered religious at all, and whether the controversy surrounding them had any significant meaning for religious freedom. As Pierard acknowledges, the issues feeding Anti-Masonry were "actually political and social in nature." Of course, the later nativist movements of the "Protestant Crusade"—anti-Catholic, anti-immigrant, and sometimes anti-Semitic—exploited evangelical religious feelings for their own purposes. And these purposes were usually more political than religious. The "proletarian fascism" of the Coughlins and the Winrods in more recent times had no quarrel with religious freedom as such. Although it certainly exploited the religious prejudices and fears of evangelical Protestants, it did so in order to attack, as Pierard says, "alien ideas," alien power, alien influence—"unAmericanism"—in the nation's life. It had more to do with the history of American society and politics, I am suggesting, than with the history of American religion; its bearing for religious freedom was indirect and, on balance, insignificant.

Turning briefly to Erling Jorstad's essay, I think it is interesting to observe, by way of contrast, that the very forces of immigration and diversity that were productive of intolerance in Pierard's view, are here viewed as nurturing the fundamental values of pluralism, denominationalism, voluntaryism, and activism, which have characterized the American tradition of religious life and liberty. I do not suggest that these interpretations are incompatible. As is so often the case in American history, the logic of *either/or* must be replaced by the logic of *both/and*. Immigration was productive of both diversity *and* intolerance, of dissent *and* coercion, of a plurality of sects, denominations, and creeds *and* the strident demand for conformity to a single national religion by various Protestant clerics. The paradox, if such it was, reminds us of Alexis de Tocqueville's coupling of freedom and equality with oppressive conformity. Yet, while the interpretations may not be incompatible, it makes a great deal of difference whether the historian chooses to emphasize one side of the reality or the other. From Pierard's perspective, Moral Majority, like the nativist movements before it, is a real and present danger and deeply disturbing. Jorstad is also worried by new deviations from "the mainstream," but unless I mistake his opinion, these movements strike him as comparatively weak and ineffectual before the massive reality of the voluntarist tradition and the legal guarantees of the First Amendment.

Jorstad is on sound grounds in viewing the tradition of church-state relations as a mixed product of rationalistic theory and the practical experience of religious pluralism. The achievement of religious freedom was owing, not to one influence or the other, but, as he says, to "that strange coalition of rationalist and pietist." Strange indeed! Rationalist and pietist united on the goal of legal disestablishment, freedom of religious conscience, and the voluntary system of religious life. But for the former— *philosophes* like Jefferson and Madison—religion was strictly an affair of the private conscience; clothed with public authority it became corrupt and oppressive, and so the public realm must be secured from its influence. For believers, on the other hand, the church, especially the Protestant church in all its denominational diversity, remained the indispensable fountainhead of religion and morality even after disestablishment; and it was the church that must be secured from the corruptions of the state—not the other way around—so that its teachings could permeate society. There were, then, two versions of what religious freedom was for, two visions—one secular in the Enlightenment mold, one theological in the evangelical Protestant mold—of what the nation should be. The fact that the Supreme Court of the United States came to adopt the secular Jeffersonian version has made a great difference in our recent history. As the legal historian Mark DeWolfe Howe once pointed out, we have generally followed the court in taking the metaphor, "a wall of separation," from Jefferson, for whom it affirmed doubt or unbelief, rather than from Roger Williams, who first used it in the seventeenth century and for whom it affirmed belief. Howe was not alone in thinking that, nevertheless, the evangelical version descending from

Williams actually had greater importance during most of our history. A "*de facto* establishment" of evangelical Protestantism prevailed, despite the legal separation, according to Howe. Religion, driven out the front door, came in again through the back door, ironically under the Jeffersonian banner. While this may be carrying a fine insight too far, it is indisputable, I think, that the American tradition of religious liberty is a dual, or forked, tradition. That is why, to reply to some of Jorstad's questions, the issues are unsettled, the historical record is unclear, and the recipe is incomplete. The evangelicals have always wanted to save not only themselves, but the nation, from sin; and the rationalists—sentinels at the "wall of separation"— have said that was none of their business. The two sides, the two versions, have been able to coexist only by virtue of agreement on the common goal of religious freedom and, at the minimum, *de jure* separation of church and state.

It is useful here to recall the crucial struggle for religious freedom in Virginia 200 years ago. It was then that the "strange coalition" was formed and the forked tradition began. The Anglican establishment had been under fire from dissenting sects, the Baptists in the lead, for several years before the Revolution. Rationalists like Jefferson and Madison, quite aside from their intellectual objections to the establishment, upbraided the clergy for failing in its moral and spiritual mission. In some parts of Virginia the Anglican Church was a hollow shell on the eve of the Revolution. Jefferson estimated that, despite its privileged status, the majority of Virginians were actually dissenters from the church. The establishment might not have long survived in any event, but it was doomed to extinction by both the necessities and the principles of the Revolution. If religious dissenters were to be expected to fight and die for the commonwealth, they could not be denied free and equal status. In a society characterized by religious pluralism and dissent, religious freedom was imperative to secure the loyalty of all to the great republic. But not everyone perceived the necessities or accepted the principles, of course. And so a long struggle ensued. The revolutionary convention that declared Virginia's independence and framed a new government left the Anglican establishment intact. The Declaration of Rights that accompanied the Constitution contained the new principle of religious freedom, however. As drafted by George Mason, the Declaration guaranteed "the fullest Toleration in the Exercise of Religion." The concept of toleration, as in the English Toleration Act previously in force in the colony, and as in John Locke's celebrated *Letter Concerning Toleration*, assumed an official and preferred religion along with the right of the state to grant or withhold favor from "dissenting" religions. This did not suit the delegate from Orange

38

County, twenty-five-year-old James Madison. He offered an amendment which changed the crucial words to "all men are equally entitled to the free exercise of religion." Religious freedom was placed upon the rational ground of natural rights, the very same ground upon which Jefferson placed American independence.

Of course, the mere declaration of principle did not disestablish the church. When the first legislature under the new constitution met in the fall of 1776, it was flooded with petitions begging for disestablishment and the end of disabilities. "These brought on the severest contest in which I have ever been engaged," Jefferson reflected many years later. He assumed the leadership of the liberal forces in the House of Delegates. (Madison had been appointed to the executive council.) After a series of legislative twists and turnings, a bill was adopted that exempted dissenters from taxes and other support of the church and temporarily suspended, though it did not abolish, levies on the members. This act also reserved decision on the question, "Whether a general assessment should not be established by law, on every one, to the support of the pastor of his choice, or whether all should be left to voluntary contributions." Here was a new issue that went beyond the fate of the established church. Always before the *establishment of religion* meant a single state church. Now, in the shadow of the doomed Anglican establishment in Virginia, it took on a new meaning: the civil support of Christian religion without preference as to sect. This rapidly became the crucial issue in the decade-long struggle in Virginia. In fact, it would become the crucial issue in several other states as well; in the case of Massachusetts it was only finally resolved in 1833.

Jefferson was disappointed in the December 1776 statute. It fell short of his own legislative resolutions and of the principles he expounded in a remarkable speech to the delegates—a speech that formed the basis of his philosophical essay on religious freedom in his book, *Notes on Virginia,* several years later. He began with a history lesson on the evils and oppressions of religious establishments. He pointed out that even in revolutionary Virginia, Baptist preachers were persecuted, and under the laws a heretic might be punished by death, a Unitarian by three years imprisonment, a free-thinker might have his children taken from him, and so on. Jefferson then posed the fundamental question: "Has the state a right to adopt an opinion in matters of religion?" Answering with a resounding negative, he pursued the argument beyond the original question of a single state church. On the premise of Lockean contract theory, men unite in government to secure those rights they cannot secure themselves. Religious conscience, being wholly private, is not one of them, and hence is not submitted to civil authority. Men are answerable for their religion solely to God. Its free exercise does no injury to others. Jefferson gave memorable expression to the doctrine: "The legitimate powers of government extend to such acts only as are injurious to others. But it does me no injury for my neighbors to say there are twenty gods or no god. It neither picks my pocket, nor breaks my leg." Regardless of the question of natural right, Jefferson went on, government intervention in the affairs of religion is harmful to religion itself. The well-known vices of the Anglican clergy in Virginia and the incompetence of that church despite its unique powers and privileges offered persuasive evidence near at hand. But throughout history, Jefferson argued, the progress of truth in religion as in science followed the march of free inquiry and private judgment against the coercion and error of civil and ecclesiastical authority. "It is error alone which needs the support of government," he said. "Truth can stand by itself." Religious differences—pluralism over uniformity—were actually beneficial to the peace and order of society. "The several sects perform the office of a *censor morum* over each other." They were equally beneficial to religion, setting up a virtuous competition among the sects and requiring them to develop their own resources rather than to depend upon external support.

These principles shaped Jefferson's Statute of Religious Freedom drafted in 1777 and first introduced in the legislature two years later. Then and for several years to come the legislature had before it alternate plans. One, Jefferson's, which was not so much a plan as it was a root-and-branch denial of any civil authority in matters of religion; the other, the general assessment plan. Neither could muster majority support. Another item on Jefferson's reform agenda, education, was essential to the new republican order he envisioned. He proposed a comprehensive plan of public education, embracing primary schools, secondary schools, and a state university. The parish church would be replaced by the local schoolhouse as the dominant moral and educational force in the community. In a sense, the common school would become the established church. Jefferson's educational plan was a landmark in the history of American education. It never came to fruition in Virginia, however. The constructive part of his reform program, as embodied in the general education bill, was defeated, while the destructive part of it, if we may so label the religion bill, would become law. A companion bill to transform the Anglican college, William and Mary, into a secular state university, was also defeated. Yet he succeeded, as a trustee of the college, in eliminating its grammar school (where pupils were taught the catechism), together with the professorship of divinity and another professorship committed to the conversion of the Indians to Christianity. Its mission was changed to the scientific study of the Indians. Anthropology replaced salvation!

40

It would be many years, of course, before Jefferson would realize his ideal of a secular state university.

The culmination of the religious controversy occurred in the years just after the Revolutionary War. In 1784, Patrick Henry, the most popular man in the government, placed himself at the head of the movement for the general assessment plan. He and his associates, primarily friends of the old church now reorganized as the Protestant Episcopal Church, argued that state support of the Christian religion and of Christian worship was essential for cultivating the public virtue upon which republican government depended. Jefferson was in France, but Madison had returned to the legislature and he led the opposition to Henry. The coalition of rationalists and sectarians was revived. Many Presbyterians remained outside, however. The famed Hanover Presbytery gave cautious endorsement to the general assessment bill. Madison remarked acidly that many of the Presbyterian clergy were "as ready to set up an establishment which is to take them in as they were to pull down that which shut them out." But for the suspicion that the bill looked primarily to propping-up the Episcopalians, the Methodists too, though not the Baptists, would probably have supported it. Madison cleverly postponed legislative action on the bill in 1784, when he could not win. The next year he rallied the coalition with his remarkable "Memorial and Remonstrance against Religious Assessments," which circulated as a petition throughout the state. A brilliant exposition of the twin principles of religious freedom and separation of church and state, the "Memorial" was founded on the rational natural rights philosophy of the Enlightenment; but, not forgetting his evangelical allies, Madison also argued that public aid and intervention subverted rather than sustained religion and was "an unhallowed perversion of the means of salvation." When the legislature convened again, the general assessment bill was quickly buried and Madison capped the climax with the enactment of Jefferson's Statute of Religious Freedom.

It was Jefferson's and Madison's philosophy on the subject that was thus written into law. The celebrated statute declared that "Almighty God hath created the mind free," "that our civil rights have no dependence on our religious opinions," that to allow government to intervene is wrong and destructive not alone of religion but of liberty itself, and finally, that "truth is great and will prevail if left to herself." The statute was an eloquent manifesto of freedom of mind, always Jefferson's primary value. It was also, more significantly for us, the theoretical and legal cornerstone of the American tradition of religious freedom. As Mr. Justice Rutledge said in 1947, using another metaphor, "The great instruments of the Virginia struggle...became warp and woof of our constitutional tradition."

41

Reflecting on that struggle in his old age, Jefferson said, "It was the universal opinion of the century preceding the last, that civil government could not stand without the prop of a religious establishment, and that the Christian religion itself would perish if not supported by a legal provision for the clergy. The experience of Virginia conspicuously corroborates the disproof of both opinions." The voluntary system succeeded better than he or anyone had expected. Religious tyranny disappeared and religion flourished. The secular Jeffersonian policy easily accommodated religious groups that accepted freedom even as many of them rejected its spirit. Rationalists coexisted with evangelicals. The price today of continued co-existence is adherence, on both sides, to the founding principles. The threat now comes primarily from the Protestant right. If it is further politicized, if it seeks further to impose its own moral and spiritual values on government and laws, if it attempts to employ the engines of state for its own purposes, then our country is destined to be wracked by deep religious controversy, and the great tradition of freedom and separation will be placed in jeopardy.

The First Amendment: Religious Neutrality or an Establishment of Secularism?
by Charles E. Rice

In his interpretive essay, "The First Amendment: Religious Neutrality or an Establishment of Secularism?" Professor Charles E. Rice of the Notre Dame Law School raises broad questions about the role of religious authority in education under the First Amendment. The Founding Fathers, he contends, did not intend to create any constitutional provision which mandated a godless society. Since the 1960s, however, the Supreme Court has veered from the founders' intentions by insisting that non-theistic religions be placed on an equal footing with Christianity in public education. For Rice, the secularism sanctioned by the court does not in fact provide neutrality in religion, but fosters a climate in education which is hostile to theistic religion. "All education is essentially religious," Rice affirms, and to deny the acceptability of propositions about God is essentially to exclude from the child's education any serious consideration of Christianity. Moreover, the court's misguided sanctioning of secularism places the state, according to Rice, in the position of denying the existence of God.

Rice challenges his readers to consider the distinction between the constitutional sanction against state establishment of any one religion and the state's requirement that no educator shall be allowed to affirm theistic convictions in the educational process. In doing so, Rice raises thought-provoking questions about the Supreme Court's interpretation of the role of religious authority in the education of American youth.

"We're no Holier for Our Holy War." This was the title of an op ed piece in the *New York Times* by Martin E. Marty, professor of the History of Modern Christianity at the University of Chicago. Dr. Marty's thesis is that what he calls "the new religious Right" is sowing discord and injustice in its claim that secular humanism has become the established religion of this land. "America may have a (sometimes creative) civil religion," Marty wrote, "but it has also gotten by as a civil society. Alongside its public religion its schools have been productive on the basis of a public philosophy." The writer G. K. Chesterton did call this "the nation with the soul of a church," but, like the other nations of the free West, it is also a nation with the soul of a nation. Arthur Mann, a University of Chicago historian, recently reminded discussants in a debate that through most of America's history, citizens did well with simpler concepts like "American ideals," and asked "whatever happened to them?" Not every aspect of every world view, science class, notion, or philosophy has to be a matter of "ultimate concern" and thus religion. Citizens can pursue religion through churches, synagogues, and, yes, tiny clubs of Secular Humanism. The religions have a right to seek influence in the free realm. "What the United States needs now is civil argument, which can resume only when the holy war scales down."

The purpose of this paper is to examine the meaning of the religion clauses of the First Amendment and to evaluate the claim that we have established some form of secularism as the national religion. The First Amendment religion clauses read: "Congress shall make no law respecting an establishment of religion, or prohibiting the free exercise thereof. . . ." The original meaning of the establishment clause is clear. Said Judge Thomas Cooley: "By establishment of religion is meant the setting up or recognition of a state church, or at least the conferring upon one church special favors and advantages which are denied to others." At the time of the American Revolution, there were at least eight states with established churches in this sense of the term. In 1791, when the Bill of Rights was adopted, there were at least four.

The evil against which the establishment clause was directed was the establishment by Congress of a particular sect or combination of sects as a direct and favored beneficiary of public

44

funds. In the words of James Madison during the debate in Congress over its adoption, "The people feared one sect might obtain a pre-eminence, or two combine together, and establish a religion to which they would compel others to conform." The Bill of Rights, however, had no application against state governments. Until the Supreme Court construed the Fourteenth Amendment to require such application, therefore, the establishment clause was a restriction only on the federal government and not on the states. Professor Edward S. Corwin summarized this point: "That is, Congress shall not prescribe a national faith, a possibility which those states with establishments of their own...probably regard with fully as much concern as those which had gotten rid of their establishments."

The establishment clause commanded impartiality on the part of government as among the various sects of theistic religions, that is, religions that profess a belief in God. But, as between theistic religions and those nontheistic creeds that do not acknowledge God, the precept of neutrality under the establishment clause did not obtain. Government, conformably to the establishment clause, could generate an affirmative atmosphere of hospitality toward theistic religion, so long as no substantial partiality was shown toward any particular theistic sect or combination of sects. Justice Joseph Story, who served on the Supreme Court from 1811 to 1845 and who was a leading Unitarian, confirmed this meaning of the First Amendment:

Probably at the time of the adoption of the Constitution, and of the first amendment to it...the general if not the universal sentiment in America was, that Christianity ought to receive encouragement from the state so far as was not incompatible with the private rights of conscience and the freedom of religious worship. An attempt to level all religions, and to make it a matter of state policy to hold all in utter indifference, would have created universal disapprobation, if not universal indignation. The real object of the amendment was not to countenance, much less to advance, Mahometanism, or Judaism, or infidelity, by prostrating Christianity; but to exclude all rivalry among Christian sects, and to prevent any national ecclesiastical establishment which should give to a hierarchy the exclusive patronage of the national government.

Logically, this means that, for purposes of the establishment clause nontheistic beliefs were not considered to be religions. Otherwise, an affirmation by government that there is a God would be a governmental preference, through the assertion of the essential truth of theism, of a combination of religious sects, i.e.,

45

those that believe in God, to the disparagement of those other religions which do not profess such a belief. On the contrary, rather than regarding theism and nontheism as merely variant religious sects within a broadly defined category of "religion," the establishment clause regarded theism as the common denominator of all religions, and nontheism it considered not to be a religion at all. Government itself could profess a belief in God, and, so long as a practical neutrality was maintained among theistic sects, the neutrality command of the establishment clause would not be breached. It is obvious, of course, that for purposes of the free exercise clause, nontheistic beliefs were regarded as religions. Atheists were as fully protected as Presbyterians in the free exercise of their beliefs. But the neutrality required by the establishment clause was neutrality among theistic creeds. The establishment clause definition of religion, therefore, was similar to that used by Chief Justice Hughes in his dissenting opinion in a 1931 case involving the eligibility of a pacifist for naturalization:

> The essence of religion is belief in a relation to God involving duties superior to those arising from any human relation....One cannot speak of religious liberty, with proper appreciation of its essential and historic significance, without assuming the existence of a belief in supreme allegiance to the will of God.

This original meaning of the religion clauses of the First Amendment was a reflection of the general Christian consensus that then existed. But that Christian consensus eventually eroded. In the 1963 decision which outlawed prayer in public schools, Justice William Brennan aptly said:

> [O]ur religious composition makes us a vastly more diverse people than were our forefathers. They knew differences chiefly among Protestant sects. Today the Nation is far more heterogeneous religiously, including as it does substantial minorities not only of Catholics and Jews but as well of those who worship according to no version of the Bible and those who worship no God at all.

As the American religious consensus changed, so, too, did the posture of government toward religion. In 1961, Roy R. Torcaso was refused a commission as a Maryland notary public because he refused to comply with the requirement of the Maryland constitution that all public officials declare their "belief in the existence of God." The Supreme Court invalidated this requirement because it unconstitutionally invaded Torcaso's "freedom of belief and religion" (*Torcaso* v. *Watkins*, 1961). In *Torcaso*, the court held that the Maryland requirement that public officials declare their belief in the existence of God was invalid because "the power and authority of the State of Maryland thus is put on the side of one particular sort of believers— those who are willing to say they believe in 'the existence of God." The court for the first time expressly declared that nontheistic beliefs are to be considered religions in the constitutional sense:

> We repeat and again reaffirm that neither a State nor the Federal Government can constitutionally force a person "to profess his belief or disbelief in any religion." Neither can constitutionally pass laws or impose requirements which aid all religions as against non-believers, and neither can aid these religions based on belief in the existence of God as against those religions founded on different beliefs.

Attached to this clause was a footnote specifying that:

> Among religions in this country which do not teach what would commonly be considered a belief in the existence of God are Buddhism, Taoism, Ethical Culture, Secular Humanism and others.

The result in the Torcaso case could be supported on free exercise of religion grounds, on the principle that it improperly infringes on an atheist's free exercise of religion to bar him from general state employment on account of his atheism. However, two years later, in the 1963 school prayer case (*Abington School District* v. *Schempp*), the Supreme Court explicitly adopted the Torcaso definition of religion as the standard of the establishment clause. Government, therefore, is now required to maintain neutrality, not among theistic sects while encouraging Christianity or theism in general, but as between the two types of religion, the theistic and the nontheistic. The court, in effect, commands government to suspend judgment on the very question of whether God exists. Justice Brennan, in his concurring opinion in the 1963 prayer case, captured the meaning of that ruling when he argued that the words "under God" in the pledge of allegiance are not necessarily unconstitutional:

> This general principle might also serve to insulate the various patriotic exercises and activities used in the public schools and elsewhere which, whatever may have been their origins, *no longer have a religious purpose or meaning*. The reference to divinity in the revised pledge of allegiance,

for example. *may merely recognize the historical fact that our Nation was believed to have been founded "under God."* Thus reciting the pledge may be no more of a religious exercise than the reading aloud of Lincoln's Gettysburg Address, which contains an allusion to the same historical fact. (Emphasis added.)

The words "under God" may therefore be retained in the pledge only if they are merely ceremonial and not to be taken seriously. Thus it would be strictly unconstitutional for the president or a public school teacher to declare as a fact that God exists. When the teacher is asked by a pupil whether the Declaration of Independence is true when it says there is a God, he cannot say yes, for that would prefer theism, and he cannot say no, for that would prefer atheism. The only answer he can give is to say that he cannot say one way or the other—that is, that he, in his official capacity in acting for the state, cannot know whether God exists. As a matter of state policy, the existence of God must be regarded as unknown or unknowable. But in principle this is a clear preference of an agnostic, secular religious creed.

For 170 years government managed to maintain a rough equilibrium in its own attitude toward religion. The initial encouragement of a common-denominator Christianity was broadened and became an encouragement of an amorphous theism. Until the 1940s the establishment clause had not been held to be strictly applicable against the states. The states were allowed to be somewhat sectarian in their encouragement of theistic religion, as evidenced by the generally Protestant character of the public schools through the early years of the twentieth century and the retention in them of such Protestant trappings as the recitation of the Lord's Prayer and the reading of the King James version of the Bible. As long as the states were not held to be strictly bound by the establishment clause of the First Amendment, there was no need for the Supreme Court to spell out exactly what would be allowed on the local level. However, once the establishment clause was strictly applied against the states, the court could no longer avoid the question whether that clause required the states and local governments to be neutral as between theism and nontheism or merely among theistic sects. In the 1962 and 1963 school prayer cases, the court ruled that every unit of government is required to maintain neutrality in its own actions between theism and nontheism. The application by the courts of this new concept of neutrality has been rigorous and logically consistent.

In 1965, the federal courts ruled that public school kindergartners, before they ate their cookies and milk, could not recite, on their own initiative, the Romper Room Grace: "God is Great,

God is Good, and we thank Him for our food. Amen." Nor could they recite a grace that said:

Thank you for the World so Sweet
Thank you for the Food we Eat,
Thank you for the Birds that Sing—
Thank you, God, for everything.

(*Stein* v. *Oshinsky,* cert. denied, 1965).

Two years later, a federal court ruled that public school kindergarten children in Illinois could not recite the latter verse even though they left the word "God" out of the last line. The court's idea was that everyone knows who "you" is—that is, God. The intent is to offer thanks to God, which is unlawful in public schools (*DeSpain* v. *DeKalb County Community School District,* cert. denied, 1968.)

Another court ruled that public high school students could not voluntarily meet in the school gymnasium before school to listen to a volunteer student read the opening "remarks" of the congressional chaplain as contained in the *Congressional Record.* The volunteer readers would "add remarks concerning such subjects as love of neighbor, brotherhood and civic responsibility. At the conclusion of the reading the students are asked to meditate for a short period of time either on the material that has been read or upon anything they desire." The court held that the congressional chaplain's "remarks" were really prayers and were therefore forbidden in public school. Apparently they are constitutional in Congress because congressmen are less susceptible to subversion by religion because they are more mature—a conclusion that is open to some doubt. Recently a federal court upheld the refusal of a public school board to allow students to conduct voluntary prayer meetings on school premises before the start of school. Even though students are allowed to form political and other secular clubs, they cannot meet for the purpose of praying. (*Brandon* v. *Board of Education of Guilderland Central School District,* 1980). And public high school football coaches have been forbidden, according to the *New York Times,* to lead their teams in a pre-game prayer. "We'll break the law," retorted one coach. "We wouldn't go out onto the field without a prayer."

Other examples could be cited to show the diligence of the courts in requiring governments at every level to suspend judgment on the existence of God.

Pursuant to this neutrality mandate, public schools must not only avoid prayers and other affirmations of the existence of God but they must also maintain a less clearly defined neutrality as well on moral questions. Thus, while a course on sex education may constitutionally present different moral views to the pupils, it may not present God's law as a binding criterion and it may not advance any of the contradictory views as morally preferable.

As a result of such rulings, a generation of public schoolers has grown to maturity without seeing the state, in the person of their teachers, affirm as a fact that there is a standard or right and wrong that is higher than the state. The question arises, of course, as to whether this suspension of judgment on the existence of God or on a moral issue is itself an implicit promotion of a secularist and relativist religion.

The mere fact that the public school's treatment of a given issue happens to coincide with the tenets of a particular religion does not mean the school is promoting that religion. Thus, the Catholic Church condemns bank robbery and so does the public school. But that does not make the public school an instrumentality of the Vatican. Proof of the argument that the public school is promoting a religion of secularism requires more than a mere coincidence of positions between the school and the secularist creed. Rather, the argument depends upon whether a nonjudgmental, secular treatment of an issue (abortion, for example) necessarily involves an affirmation, expressly or by standard exclusion, of the irrelevancy of the supernatural. It then must be asked whether to affirm the irrelevancy of the supernatural is necessarily to favor the position of some form of secular religion. It is not unreasonable to describe such teaching as an implicit affirmation of a position that, in its relativism and its effort to interpret life without reference to the supernatural, is authentically religious. It is true that the establishment clause of the First Amendment embodied a restrictive definition of religion that included only theistic creeds. But that limited usage of the term, "religion," has now been supplanted in Supreme Court decisions by the broader Torcaso definition that includes nontheistic as well as theistic beliefs within the meaning of the term. It is obvious that this broader definition is more in accord with reality than is the narrow, theistic definition intended by the framers of the establishment clause. Indeed, the broader definition was used elsewhere in the First Amendment itself, in the free exercise clause which protected the free exercise of religion by atheists and agnostics as well as by theists.

One curious feature of the present debate is the tendency in some quarters to assume that an affirmation of God is a religious statement while a denial of Him has nothing at all to do with the subject. On the contrary, both positions are religious, involving the affirmative and negative of the same question. The accuracy of this broad definition of religion is particularly evident in the field of education. Professor Edward Barrett described jurisprudence as an exercise in "ultimatology," a term which can be applied as well to education. At least on the elementary and secondary levels, every educational enterprise involves a choice—whether explicit or implicit—of an ultimate criterion. It is a choice of a god. This position is strongly maintained by some theoreticians and activists in the contemporary Christian school movement. Their position is well taken. If it were not for the need for advocates of public education to make the debater's points required by the Supreme Court's fiction that the exclusion of the supernatural is not a religious position, it would be generally conceded that education is religious. "The essence of education," wrote Alfred North Whitehead, "is that it be religious." This point, among others, was missed by the Supreme Court in the 1963 school prayer case in which the court said "the State may not establish a religion of secularism in the sense of affirmatively opposing or showing hostility to religion, thus 'preferring those who believe in no religion over those who do believe.'" (*Abington School District* v. *Schempp,* 1963). The religious character of nontheistic creeds can be seen from *Humanist Manifestoes I* and *II.* In 1933, *Humanist Manifesto I,* a statement of secularist beliefs, was issued by a group of public figures, including John Dewey, the educational philosopher. In 1973, an updated and similar *Humanist Manifesto II* was issued by 120 religious leaders, philosophers, social scientists, and others. (The signers included Andrei D. Sakharov, the dissident Russian physicist; Paul Blanshard, a leading proponent of the separation of religion from the state; Professor Sidney Hook of New York University; Dr. Francis Crick, the discoverer of the structure of the DNA molecule; Dr. Alan Guttmacher, president of the Planned Parenthood Federation of America; Lawrence Lader, chairman of the National Association for Repeal of Abortion Laws; Professor B. F. Skinner of Harvard University; Jerome Nathanson, chairman of the New York Society of Ethical Culture; Vashti McCollum, the plaintiff in *McCollum* v. *Board of Education* and former president of the American Humanist Association; Professor Chaim Perelman of the University of Brussels; and others. *Humanist Manifesto II* is useful here for its demonstration of the ultimate character of humanist belief and the practical as well as the theoretical inconsistency between the humanist position and the Christian faith, which includes an affirmation of absolute truths derived from divine revelation. The manifesto proclaimed:

> We believe that traditional dogmatic or authoritarian religions that place revelation, God, ritual or creed above human needs and experience do a disservice to the human species.
>
> Promises of immortal salvation or fear of eternal damnation are both illusory and harmful. They distract humans from present concerns, from self-actualization and from

rectifying social injustices.

We affirm that moral values derive their source from human experience. Ethics is autonomous and situational, needing no theological or ideological sanction. Ethics stems from human need and interest. To deny this distorts the whole basis of life.

We strive for the good life, here and now.

. . . .

In the area of sexuality, we believe that intolerant attitudes, often cultivated by orthodox religions and puritanical cultures, unduly repress sexual conduct. The right to birth control, abortion and divorce should be recognized. While we do not approve of exploitive, denigrating forms of sexual expression, neither do we wish to prohibit, by law or social sanction, sexual behavior between consenting adults.

To enhance freedom and dignity, the individual must experience a full range of civil liberties in all societies. This includes . . . a recognition of an individual's right to die with dignity, euthanasia and the right to suicide.

The religious character of secular humanism can be seen most clearly in the public school environment. The public schools in the beginning were not secular. They were essentially non-denominational Protestant schools. It was in reaction to this condition that Catholic parochial schools were first established. Today, the public schools profess neutrality in religion, but the fact is that no school can be neutral vis-à-vis God. As Patrick Cardinal O'Boyle commented:

> Of course, it may be argued that the public schools need not favor any particular religion or religion at all, for they can proceed on strictly humanistic, pragmatic and secular conceptions. But this is precisely the point. To proceed in this way is itself to establish a religion—secular humanism—and to favor this religion over all others. . . .

Historically, John Dewey, who has so much to do with progressive education, which deeply affected the philosophical functions of our present public schools, spoke of his own beliefs, which were a form of secular humanism, in religious terms. In a statement first published in 1897, entitled 'My Pedagogic Creed,' Dewey said that in shaping children as members of secular society the teacher is 'always the prophet of the true God and the usherer in of the kingdom of God.'

For Dewey, the true God is not the Holy Trinity, but is the human community; the true kingdom of God is not heaven, but is the secular city perfected by applied science. Dewey

52

claimed that public schools, in contributing to the realization of this ideal, would be doing a genuinely religious work, more so indeed than could be done with all of the paraphernalia of traditional religion.

The public school is a religious institution whose creed is secularism. As Paul Blanshard, a signer of the *Humanist Manifesto II*, recently observed:

I think that the most important factor moving us toward a secular society has been the educational factor. Our schools may not teach Johnny to read properly, but the fact that Johnny is in school until he is sixteen tends to lead toward the elimination of religious superstition. The average American child now acquires a high-school education, and this militates against Adam and Eve and all other myths of alleged history....

...When I was one of the editors of *The Nation* in the twenties, I wrote an editorial explaining that golf and intelligence were the two primary reasons that men did not attend Church. Perhaps I would now say golf and a high-school diploma.

Ideas have consequences. And it is not unreasonable to conclude that a steady classroom diet of suspended judgment and *laissez faire* on moral issues can influence the students' own religious belief away from an acknowledgment of an objective law of God and can amount to an overall promotion of secularism. There is logic in the following comment by a writer in *The American Atheist:*

And how does a god die? Quite simply because all his religionists have been converted to another religion, and there is no one left to make children believe they need him.

Finally, it is irresistible—we must ask how we can kill the god of Christianity. We need only insure that our schools teach only secular knowledge; that they teach children to constantly examine and question all theories and truths put before them in any form; and that they teach that nothing is proven by the number of persons who believe a thing to be true. If we could achieve this, god would indeed be shortly due for a funeral service.

This is the language of warfare. And it is appropriate. Every educational system, as with every legal system, has to have a God, an ultimate authority. If that authority is not the real God, it will be another, whether the consensus, the Supreme Court, the autonomous individual conscience, or whatever. In the educational arena, the conflict between the theistic and nontheistic religious views is irreconcilable. Nor is it possible to effect any authentic coexistence of the two. The Supreme Court, for example, emphasizes that it is constitutional to teach *about* religion, so long as the public school makes no affirmation that any particular religion is true. But this pretended suspension of judgment is itself a judgment and is properly seen by Christian and other parents as a contradiction of their beliefs. The impressive growth of excellent, Bible-oriented Christian schools reflects the intensity of this conviction.

Religious warfare tends to be aggressive warfare. It is therefore not surprising that Christian and other parents have strenuously opposed the manifestations of humanist religion in public school programs. And it is not surprising that state education authorities have just as strenuously opposed the efforts of Christian parents to form schools which are independent of those authorities.

The efforts of objecting parents against humanist religion in the public schools have been singularly unsuccessful. Public school authorities are not required by the courts to excuse objecting pupils from sex education and other programs to which they offer religious objections. Whether the pupils will be excused is a matter for the discretion of the school authorities. And, of course, the courts have rejected efforts by parents to remove sex education programs entirely from the curriculum. The decisive factor here, as far as the establishment clause is concerned, is the tendency of the courts to treat secular public education, including sex education, as authentically neutral and not itself religious. This prevailing myth was articulated by Justice Jackson in 1947:

> Our public school, if not a product of Protestantism, at least is more consistent with it than with the Catholic culture and scheme of values. It is a relatively recent development dating from about 1840. It is organized on the premise that secular education can be insulated from all religious teaching so that the school can inculcate all needed temporal knowledge and also maintain a strict and lofty neutrality as to religion. The assumption is that after the individual has been instructed in worldly wisdom he will be better fitted to choose his religion.

Nor is the solution to be found in an effort by the public schools to teach generalized morality. For example, the minimum standards for Ohio elementary schools which were involved in *State* v. *Whisner* (1976) included such moralisms as "Democracy is based on such beliefs as the integrity of the individual, equality of opportunity, man's rationality, man's morality, man's ability to govern himself and to solve his problems co-operatively." The objecting Christian parents properly rejected this sort of moralizing because it is "man-centered" and "places all its emphasis on the present life, with no provision for the teaching of after-life." For those who object to public education as permeated with secular humanism, no solution is offered by the schools' efforts to teach morality in a way that avoids such questions as whether God or some other is the source of rights and duties and whether there is an afterlife.

Another manifestation of the hostility of public education to Christian belief is the reluctance of the courts to require public school administrators to allow the formation of Bible clubs on the same terms applicable to political, civic, and other clubs.

When Christian parents have formed their own schools, they have often found that state education authorities are aggressive in their efforts to impose on those Christian schools the same secular standards that apply to the public schools. There is no question but that such schools are subject to appropriate fire, safety, and health regulations. The controversy instead involves accreditation. The root of the word "accreditation" is "credo"—"I believe." Since education is inherently religious and since the standards of the state are irreconcilably in conflict with their own, the objecting parents properly regard the submission to state accreditation as a submission to a false religion. And they are correct in that view. With respect to long-established private school systems, including the Catholic, state accreditation has generally been a benign process. And some of those systems, especially the Catholic, have been persistent advocates of public support even at the price of some secularization of those private schools. When textbooks are provided at public expense to Catholic school pupils, for example, they are secular textbooks approved for use in the public schools. The newer Christian schools, however, refuse to compromise the integrity of their educational mission. They refuse accreditation and they refuse the application to their schools of state educational standards, including teacher certification, curriculum requirements, competency testing, etc. It is argued that the state's interest in promoting literacy among the citizenry justifies state regulation of private schools. State supervision, it is argued, is necessary to ensure that the church-related schools do their basic educational job. However, the academic performance of the public schools hardly supports that contention. The dominance of public education has not brought about an increase in either the literacy or the civic competence of its beneficiaries. It is worth considering that *The Federalist Papers* were published in the popular press and were written for the average, church-school educated citizen in New York, including the rural areas. One may speculate as to how many high school seniors could read them intelligently today. The Christian schools have won some notable victories in this continuing controversy, principally through the efforts of William B. Ball, the foremost constitutional lawyer in the area. But the issue is far from settled.

The root issue in this matter of education is hardly discussed at all. In view of the reality that all education is religious, it is clear that the public schools themselves are unconstitutional as a violation of the neutrality mandated by the establishment clause. This is so whether we view that clause as originally intended or as later construed by the Supreme Court. Referring to the efforts of objecting parents to prove that public school programs violate the establishment clause, Mr. Ball commented, "They may have some problems of proof in nailing down the charge that a particular program is 'Secular Humanist' but those are merely problems of proof. The reality is plainly there in many identifiable programs. On their Establishment Clause argument, the complainants are home free."

We tend to forget that public education is a relative latecomer on the American scene. One positive result of the current controversy is an increased willingness to address the issue of its basic legitimacy under the First Amendment. Dr. Martin E. Marty, in the statement quoted at the beginning of this paper, expressed the hope that what he called the "Holy War" could be toned down by a return to a common affirmation of "American ideals." It is apparent, however, that the school issue is forcing us to more basic conclusions. And this is a welcome development. For the major difficulties in this area arise from the assumption by the state of the essentially religious responsibility of education.

Religious Advocacy and Religious Legislation:
A Constitutional Paradox
by Frederick Schauer

Professor Frederick Schauer of the Marshall-Wythe School
of Law at the College of William and Mary agrees with Professor
Rice that the First Amendment has been used to separate religion
from the realm of politics, but he disagrees rather sharply with
Rice's conviction that the Supreme Court has misconstrued the
original intentions of the Founding Fathers. Schauer's essay is
concerned with the court's tests of the legitimacy of Congressional legislation which confronts a First Amendment challenge.
Says Schauer, the courts will allow religiously motivated legislation only if there is a clear secular justification for its enactment.
Hence, legislators need not disregard their religious convictions
when they vote in the chambers of government, but they would be
better advised to cloak their rationale for legislation not in
theological propositions, but in secular terms. Schauer approves
of this secular test and seems to believe that it is in keeping with
the best historical understanding of the founders' intentions. In
"Religious Advocacy and Religious Legislation: A Constitutional
Paradox," Schauer looks at the interpretation of the First
Amendment in a very different way than does Professor Rice.

The recent flurry of activity in the political arena by religious organizations presents a substantial constitutional paradox. This paradox implicates not only the frequently conflicting mandates of the two different religion clauses of the First Amendment to the Constitution, but also the free speech clause as well. It is this tension between the constitutional requirement of religious neutrality, implicit in the establishment clause, and protection of religious political activity, equally implicit in the free exercise and free speech clauses, that I wish to explore. Such an inquiry seems long overdue, because much of the contemporary debate over the propriety of religious political activity has generated far more heat than light. Those who oppose the entry of religious groups and religious leaders into the political sphere have often cried "separation of church and state" in a reflexive manner, suggesting by their remarks that there is something at least unseemly and probably unconstitutional about political activity by religious organizations. This view, however, ignores the import of the free speech and free exercise clauses, for it would be totally implausible to imagine that religious groups, solely by virtue of their particular perspective, are to be excluded from participation in the marketplace of ideas. But supporters of religious political activity have just as egregiously ignored the problems under the establishment clause, appearing at times to hold the position that if some particular piece of legislation serves an important religious purpose, then that fact alone is a sufficient condition to justify its enactment into law.

Against the background of this wholesale oversimplification of the difficulty and complexity of the issues involved, I want to begin by setting out, in what to some may be a rather rudimentary presentation, the current state of the law, without yet making specific reference to the particular theme of this paper. It is very difficult to know where to go unless you first know where you are coming from. Having outlined the constitutional framework, I will then attempt to show that religious political activity, although itself constitutionally protected, may nevertheless increase the likelihood that legislation based on those religious arguments will be held unconstitutional.

Under the establishment clause of the First Amendment,

now taken to be applicable to the states as well as to the federal government (*Everson* v. *Board of Education,* 1947), it is impermissible for a government to make laws "respecting an establishment of religion." As with most of the other crucially important and frequently litigated clauses of the Constitution, the particular words of the text of the establishment clause do not take us very far in answering most of the hard questions that arise in its interpretation and application. Nor is original intent as gleaned from historical documents substantially more helpful; although, if we look carefully at the writings of Madison and Jefferson, the leading architects of the clause, we see that Jefferson's metaphor of the "wall of separation" between church and state is by no means an exaggerated statement either of his views or those of Madison.

In the face of such relatively indeterminate textual and historical guidance, the Supreme Court has been compelled to develop finer tools for establishment clause analysis. Whether the tools thus far developed are adequate to the task is highly debatable, especially if one looks at the almost random pattern of the school financing cases, but it is at least settled now that establishment clause analysis requires a three-part inquiry. (*Wald* v. *Tax Commission,* 1970).

Under the first branch of this inquiry, legislation (as well as any other form of governmental action) is constitutionally invalid if it lacks a secular legislative purpose. Thus if governmental action is designed or intended to serve a religious purpose, it is unconstitutional as a contravention of the establishment clause, and this is so whether the governmental action seeks to aid one religion in particular, or religion in general. (*Everson* and *Abington School District* v. *Schempp,* 1963). It is this prong of the establishment clause test that compels the constitutional invalidity of prayers in the public schools (*Abington* and *Stone* v. *Graham,* 1980), because the very notion of a prayer can and does serve no purpose except the religious. But it is important to remember that a secular purpose can exist even in the presence of some incidental service to religious goals as well, and the courts will not find a lack of secular purpose when a secular purpose coexists with a religious purpose. A good example is the Sunday Closing cases (*McGowan* v. *Maryland,* 1961), in which the Supreme Court found that the religious origins and even current religious orientation of the laws were insufficient for a finding of unconstitutionality in the face of a current secular purpose to provide a uniform day of rest. The principle (if not the application) in these cases is difficult to deny, because most of our laws have, if we trace their origins back far enough, some religious foundation. But it would be bizarre to suggest the laws prohibiting murder are unconstitutional because of the religious mandate in the Ten Commandments that "Thou shalt not kill," and this is because *present* justification for laws prohibiting murder is secular rather than religious.

Under the second branch of the establishment clause inquiry, governmental action is impermissible where it has, even in the absence of a religious purpose, a principle or primary *effect* that advances or inhibits religion (*Abington*). Government action that in practice serves mainly to aid religion is as invalid as governmental action specifically intended to reach that end. But in most of the cases in which there is a primary effect of advancing religion, such as a prohibition on teaching evolution in the public schools, there has been a religious purpose as well, and instances of effect alone being sufficient for invalidation are rare (*Epperson* v. *Arkansas*, 1968).

Finally, governmental action is invalid under the establishment clause if it fosters an excessive entanglement between government and religion (*Lemon* v. *Kurtzman*, 1971, and *Meek* v. *Pittinger*, 1975). If the law in question would involve the state or its officials in determining the truth of religious doctrine or in applying religious standards, as when a court is asked to decide between different factions within a religion (*Serbian Eastern Orthodox Church* v. *Milivojevich*, 1976), or when a governmental agency would be forced to supervise or examine in detail the methods of instruction in a religious school, as in some of the school financing cases, the wall of separation becomes an illusion. This is often more to the detriment of religion than to the state, and the governmental action is once again not permitted to stand.

Thus, to recapitulate, governmental action is impermissible under the establishment clause if it *either* has no secular purpose, or if it has a primary effect of advancing or inhibiting religion, or if it causes an excessive entanglement between government and religion.

In order to complete the legal background for the problem I wish to focus on, we must look now at the free speech and free exercise of religion clauses of the First Amendment. Although in most cases these two clauses serve rather different purposes, I see no reason to distinguish them in this particular context, for here they operate in tandem toward the same end. And that end, immovably entrenched in our constitutional law, is that religious speech is not and cannot be less deserving of constitutional protection than any other form of speech (*Cantwell* v. *Connecticut*, 1940). Indeed, much of classical free speech theory, especially the works of John Milton, John Locke, and John Stuart Mill, was directed specifically toward the issue of free expression of religious sentiments. And many of the cases that form the core of modern free speech doctrine in constitutional law are cases involving religious speech, most notable among them being the large number of cases dealing with the free speech rights of the Jehovah's Witnesses (e.g., *Cantwell* and *Lovell* v. *Griffin*, 1938). Among the central principles of contemporary free speech doctrine is a strong, albeit not absolute, aversion to content regulation, meaning that the extent of free speech protection may not, except in rare circumstances, turn on the subject the speaker wishes to discuss, nor on the speaker's particular point of view with respect to that subject (*Police Department of Chicago* v. *Mosley*, 1972). Although the positive values of speech are undoubtedly great, the protection of freedom of speech is in many respects based on negative considerations, particularly a distrust of governmental selection among speakers or among ideas. As we can see both from history and from looking at much of the contemporary world, governmental selection among speech and speakers entails grave risks that distinctions will be drawn far more on the basis of the personal interests of the governors than on the legitimate interests of government. In order to avoid this greater risk, we have left the selection to a relatively unconstrained marketplace, recognizing that this too is not without risks. Thus we have erected a system in which Billy Graham is as free to discuss religion as Tom Wicker is to discuss politics, and in which Jerry Falwell is as free to urge the truth of his religious beliefs as Madeline Murray O'Hair is to condemn as false all religious doctrine.

Although the phenomenon is quite common in practice, people do not usually *intend* to talk only to themselves. They want others to listen to what they have to say, and hope that those listeners will be in some way affected, such as by being shocked, offended, aroused, excited, provoked, or persuaded. And when we look at this last listed potential purpose of speech—persuasion—and combine it with the well-established foundation of free speech theory that citizens have a right to criticize the action of government so that the government may listen, or be replaced, we are forced to the conclusion, nowhere reflected in the case law because of its very obviousness, that politically oriented speech from a religious perspective is as strongly protected as politically oriented speech from any other perspective. And this is a very strong protection indeed. Some types of speech, such as commercial advertising, may be said to lie at the fringes of the First Amendment, but it is clear that speech directed towards political matters, including not only politics in a narrow partisan sense but also any potential subject of legislation, is at the central core of the First Amendment, and may thus be restricted only under the narrowest and most compelling of circumstances (*Brandenburg* v. *Ohio*, 1969, and *Hess* v. *Indiana*, 1973).

And herein lies the paradox. If, for example, a religious

leader speaks out on why, from a religious point of view, a particular piece of legislation is desirable, or necessary, and does so with the intention that a legislature will be persuaded by his arguments, his speech is unquestionably protected by the First Amendment. But if the legislature (assuming for the sake of simplicity a legislature of a single mind), persuaded by the arguments of that religious leader, enacts the legislation he proposes for precisely the religious reasons he puts forth, and if a court can discover that purpose and finds no secular purpose, then the religious purpose behind the legislation is sufficient by itself to invalidate the legislation as a violation of the establishment clause. This in itself need be no cause for surprise. For as long as the principles of freedom of speech protect the right of a citizen to urge the desirability, or even the necessity, of violation of the law (*Brandenburg*), then those same principles protect the right of a citizen to urge the enactment of unconstitutional laws. Although the citizen is virtually unrestrained in what he can say, or advocate, the government is substantially more restrained in what it can *do*. And although it is by no means necessarily the case that religious advocacy leads to legislation with an unconstitutionally religious purpose, such advocacy may increase the likelihood of that result. In this sense the more successful the religious advocate is in his advocacy, the greater the risk that the resultant legislation will fail to pass constitutional muster.

Let us look more closely at the problem, first from the point of view of the religious advocate. To the extent that people wish legislation that is explicitly and necessarily religious, such as required prayer in the public schools or prohibitions on the teaching of evolution, the paradox I am discussing is of only peripheral importance, for such explicitly religious legislation could be constitutionally permissible only if there were a major overhaul of existing establishment clause doctrine. Only with a tremendous expansion of the now narrow circumstances under which a state may specifically put its force behind religion could such legislation be acceptable, and this is not the place to delve into either the possibility, or the strategy, for such a constitutional revolution. But more commonly, people with strong religious feelings advocate the passage of legislation that is possibly but not necessarily supported by a religious justification. Laws against murder are an example, because they can be justified as an embodiment of one of the Ten Commandments, a religious document, or just as a means of avoiding or deterring the unpleasant circumstance of people killing each other. The Sunday Closing cases I mentioned previously are another example, and the Supreme Court's failure to use the establishment clause in the abortion cases except to reject its applicability is recognition that objection to abortion need not be religiously based in a narrow sense (*Harris* v. *McRae*, 1980).

Thus, a secular justification for legislation can be a practical, economic, or utilitarian justification; or it can be a moral justification. For we have recognized that morality is not the exclusive province of religion, and laws serving the goals of morality are not necessarily religious in the establishment clause sense. There is such a thing as secular morality, which we can see by the fact that many people with varied or no religious beliefs are still willing to condemn as immoral killing, lying, stealing, and racial or gender discrimination.

Given that many laws can therefore be justified on either religious or secular grounds, and that some secular justification must be present for constitutional validity, the religious advocate in the political arena must pick his audience. If he wishes to address the population at large, or some religious segment of the population, he may couch his appeals in specifically religious terms. But if, instead, he wishes to address those who make and enforce the laws, and if he wishes those laws to survive a constitutional challenge, he would be better advised to couch his appeal in secular terms. For when a law is challenged on establishment clause grounds, the courts will try to find a secular justification. In some cases the courts may identify a secular purpose even if none appears in the legislative history, but this makes things much less certain. If an advocate of legislation can provide a secular justification, and can attempt to have that justification form the explicit foundation of the legislation, the more likely it is that the courts will accept the secular justification.

The same lesson applies in terms of the point of view of the individual legislator. There is of course no bar, nor could there be, consistent with the free exercise clause, to the election of legislators with religious beliefs. But most of us live our lives in several different roles, and the same applies to the legislator. Under our constitutional system, being a legislator is to hold a secular position, and thus the legislator is mandated by the Constitution to approve only that legislation that can be justified on secular grounds. Where an appeal is made for legislation on religious grounds, it is incumbent on the legislator, if he favors the legislation, to attempt to construct a secular justification for that legislation, recognizing that such a justification may still be a moral justification. And if he takes his responsibilities seriously, he must be consistently faithful to that secular principle. All of the talk about how the teaching of theories other than Darwinian evolution is justifiable on secular grounds because the Darwinian theory is not verifiable is just that—talk—because in no other area of education do advocates of teaching creationism, scientific or otherwise, advocate legislation to require the teaching of alternate theories. Modern philosophy of science tends to reject the premise that *any* theory is verifiable; they are only falsifiable. But even if this were not the case, a secular justification would only be accepted if there were some evidence that that secular justification was uniformly applied. To apply what is claimed to be a secular justification—discuss all points of view—only in the area in which the alternative thesis comes from the Bible is to expose the purported secular justification as a sham.

It should by now be apparent that the courts are faced with an enormously difficult task in determining whether legislation has that secular purpose necessary for the legislation to survive an establishment clause attack. Questions of legislative intent, motive, and purpose are always difficult, but they are an inextricable part of our constitutional law. When a court faced with this difficult task, perhaps especially difficult in this area, of trying to determine the purpose of legislation looks to see whether that purpose is religious or secular, it can look to many sources. Although the Supreme Court has not been consistent on this, it has on occasion looked to statements made outside of the legislature as well as to those made within it in seeking to discover legislative purpose (*Epperson*). When statements within and without the legislature are explicitly religious, it is easier to find a religious purpose and harder to find a secular one. And in this case the likelihood is greater that an establishment clause attack will be upheld. The lesson for the religious advocate in the political arena, therefore, is that such advocacy has the possibility of being counterproductive. The more that legislation is advocated on specifically religious grounds, the greater the risk that the resultant legislation will be found to violate the establishment clause. The religious advocate who is interested in results will, when he enters the political arena, leave his religious oratory at home.

The "Holy" Hedge: Mutual Co-existence under the First Amendment
by Leonard S. Rubenstein

Leonard S. Rubenstein, President of the American Civil Liberties Union of Virginia, suggests that both Professors Rice and Schauer have overestimated the First Amendment's success in separating church and state. The assertion that it provides a "total shield between religion and state" distorts the historical reality that there have always been ways to get around the "wall of separation." Rubenstein sees the First Amendment as a hedge with numerous holes through which it is possible to pass with alacrity. His essay is entitled "The 'Holy' Hedge: Mutual Co-existence under the First Amendment."

American history is punctuated by periods of religious revivalism, each one of which raises anew the relationship between church and state. Professors Rice and Schauer address that relationship in its constitutional context, the establishment clause. The very first words of the Bill of Rights state the principle with which constitutional specialists grapple: "Congress shall make no law respecting an establishment of religion...." The key concept is really "how religious a polity may we be."

One view of the church-state relations issue, taken by Professor Schauer, is that any political advocacy in religious terms or with religious underpinnings is invariably tainted, and risky as well: if the legislature takes the religious argument seriously, the legislation is an enactment of a particular sectarian view and hence unconstitutional. Practical advice to the zealot is always to make his appeal to secular interests.

Professor Rice appears at the opposite end of the spectrum. For him, many of the central issues of our time cannot seriously be discussed without taking a religious position or at least one based on a particular religious (or anti-religious) set of values. The state sponsored prohibition (or so he claims) on addressing inherently religious issues in religious terms results in a new religion of secularism.

These disparate views, however, share a common, and, I believe, mistaken view of the establishment clause which leads to these rather extreme conclusions—conclusions which conflict with our everyday experience as well as constitutional thinking. They share a vision that sees the establishment clause, as interpreted by the courts, as a total shield between religion and state.

I will consider Rice's view first, not only because it is more extreme, but because it more clearly illustrates the problems of an absolutist view of the establishment clause, leading to the rather bizarre view that public education is unconstitutional. As I understand his paper, Rice makes two points. First, he says that the original meaning and interpretation of the establishment clause permitted governmental support for theism, what he calls the "Christian consensus." Second, he argues that the modern view of the clause, which rejects sponsorship of any sectarian group or groups, has had the opposite effect: it has established another religion, godless and secular. Although he does not explicitly say so, the only consistent reading of his paper is to say that we must either "return" to established Christianity or eliminate the powerful role of inherently anti-theistic secularism from public institutions.

We need not make such an unhappy choice. His first argument has little support. Despite some ambiguity in the framers' intent, the theory he advances has been repudiated by the Supreme Court each of the many times it has been raised in the court. (*Abington School District* v. *Schempp*, 1963; *Everson* v. *Board of Education*, 1964). And for good reason. Jefferson and Madison, whose influence over the clause cannot be doubted, both vigorously opposed any government support for the theistic religion which Rice sees as compatible with the clause's prohibitions. Jefferson held the more radical view: it was he who coined the (often misleading) metaphor of a "wall" between church and state. Madison, though, squarely answered Rice's argument that the framers intended to support Christianity generally in his eloquent statement of religious freedom, the "Memorial and Remonstrance" of 1784.

The "Memorial" was written in response to a bill in the Virginia General Assembly which would have supported the "Christian consensus." It authorized a tax for the support of Christian teachers of any sect designated by the taxpayer. Madison's vigorous opposition not only defeated the bill, but left us with an articulation of the meaning of "establishment" wholly at odds with the position Rice asserts. Madison saw the spectre of coercion and persecution in support for any group, however broadly defined, and specifically rejected support for a "Christian consensus."

> Who does not see that the same authority which can establish Christianity in exclusion of all other religions may establish with the same ease any particular sect of Christians, in exclusion of all other sects? That same authority which can force a citizen to contribute three pence only of his property for the support of any one establishment, may force him to conform to any other establishment in all cases whatsoever?

Madison knew of what he spoke: Baptists were jailed in Culpeper in the mid-1770s and Catholics were denied full legal protection in many of the colonies. The Christian "consensus" is as mythical as Davy Crockett's exploits.

This understanding has remained a part of the establishment clause since—Justice Story notwithstanding. Certainly as early

67

as 1871 the Supreme Court admonished, "The law knows no heresy, and is committed to the support of no dogma, the establishment of no sect." (*Watson v. Jones*, 1871). The golden age never existed.

Rice then turns to the modern era, where he sees the establishment clause turned inside out: the prohibition of state religion and the establishment of state anti-religion. His position is of the "if you are not for me, you are against me" variety: a government that does not affirmatively stand for certain religious propositions—particularly in its educational institutions—is, given the nature of contemporary thought, anti-religious.

There are rather clear difficulties with this argument. It is by now rather commonly accepted that "religion" must be defined differently for purposes of the First Amendment's free exercise and its establishment clause. While we wish to protect, under the free exercise clause, any set of beliefs, however wacky, which even resemble religion for the purposes of liberty to pray to the god (or anti-god) of one's choice, such an expansive definition will not do for the establishment clause. For that would mean that any time the state established a controversial policy which happened to embody or represent the "religious" beliefs of a particular group, and was not universally accepted, it could be accused of "establishing" that religion.

Under Rice's view of secular humanism, for example, any legislation whose intent was to protect or enhance equality or human freedom could be condemned as an establishment clause violation. Rice himself recognizes the distinction, in arguing that atheism may be "religion" for the free exercise purposes but not for establishment clause purposes. The "establishment" argument won't wash.

Moreover, when there is a clash between secular and religious values in public affairs, they cannot be accorded equal weight. That, after all, is what the establishment clause is all about—a choice of secularism. Rice's prime example, public schools, illustrates this. They foster civic values and may engender doubt in religious matters or lead to questioning sectarian beliefs. But that is part of the necessary tension in a society where religion and government have been separated and where the function of a public school is "to train American citizens in an atmosphere free of parochial, or separatist influences of any sort—an atmosphere in which children may assimilate a heritage common to all American groups and religions. This heritage is neither theistic nor atheistic, but simply civil and patriotic. That cannot be establishing any 'religion.'"

Nevertheless, Rice's argument has some appeal, especially his most provocative claim: that certain issues of public importance cannot be discussed without taking a position, implicit or explicit, on the existence of God; that by excluding religion from such discussion there is an affirmative denial of God; and that the result is an establishment of religion. That position, I think, can be answered by what I have already said. But I also want to answer what I perceive to be his most serious concern, the interpretation of the establishment clause to hinder religion.

My response—and here the argument applies to Professor Schauer as well—is that the premise of his argument—the absolute exclusion of religion from the state—is mistaken. The clause is not inflexible (though many would like it so); it leaves an enormous amount of room for religion. Only those overtly sectarian practices—or actions directly assisting such practices—closely associated with a particular and identifiable set of religious beliefs have ever been seen as establishment clause violations: Bible readings, aid to parochial schools, the prohibition on teaching the theory of evolution because it conflicts with fundamentalist Christianity.

Justice Goldberg put it this way in *Abington School District* v. *Schempp:*

> Neither government nor this Court can or should ignore the significance of the fact that a vast portion of our people believe in and worship God and that many of our legal, political and personal values derive historically from religious teachings. Government must inevitably take cognizance of the existence of religion and, indeed, under certain circumstances, the First Amendment may require it to do so.

Justice Douglas went even further—further indeed than many constitutional scholars would permit, when he wrote an opinion for the Court upholding release time in public schools for religious instruction:

> We are a religious people whose institutions presuppose a Supreme Being. We guarantee the freedom of worship as one chooses. We make room for as wide a variety of beliefs and creeds as the Spiritual needs of man deem necessary. We sponsor an attitude on the part of government that shows no partiality to any one group and that lets each flourish according to the zeal of its adherents and the appeal of its dogma. When the state encourages religious authorities by adjusting the schedule of public events to sectarian needs, it follows the best of our traditions. For it then respects the religious nature of our people and accommodates the public service to their spiritual needs. (*Zorach* v. *Clausen,* 1952).

Rhetoric this may be, but it expresses the depth of ambivalence in separation of church and state. That ambivalence is also reflected in what would otherwise be a hodgepodge of establishment clause decisions permitting certain kinds of state aid for religious schools, Sunday blue laws, and tax exemptions for churches. The establishment clause is not Jefferson's wall, but a bushy hedge, which can be crawled through, around and under. If, as Rice claims, secular society promotes a viewpoint inimical to traditional theistic religion (and I am conceding this only for the purposes of discussion), it still leaves ample room for religion. Schauer's zealot need not leave his religion at home. I think one contemporary example of this point will help, and will also serve to illustrate the differences I have with Schauer's view of the establishment clause.

My example is one both authors refer to, the divisive issue of abortion. In the case of *McRae* v. *Harris*, plaintiffs challenged the Hyde Amendment, which denies Medicaid-funded abortions to indigent women. They compiled impressive proof, based on the testimony of dozens of theologians, political scientists, sociologists, and religion and opinion analysts, that attitudes toward the legality and morality of abortion were based fundamentally on religious beliefs. Anyone reading the briefs of the plaintiffs—or the findings of the trial court—cannot help but conclude that the issues at stake were fundamentally religious in nature, that the debate about them was conducted in theological terms, and that the fervor of the advocacy was out of proportion to merely "political" issues.

Given these facts, and the long tradition that the courts ought not to embroil themselves in an issue which might encourage "political divisiveness related to religious belief and practice," (*Committee for Public Education* v. *Nyquist*, 1973), one might have expected the plaintiffs to prevail. Particularly so when the plaintiffs relied squarely on *Epperson* v. *Arkansas*, where the Supreme Court held the prohibition of the teaching of evolution to violate the establishment clause: "fundamentalist sectarian conviction was and is the law's reason for existence." (*Epperson* v. *Arkansas*, 1968). The argument had a certain logic: the plaintiffs had proved that the Hyde Amendment, like the "monkey laws," involved a wholesale and deliberate attempt to impose a certain religious view of the world on society at large. This was not the mere coincidence of religious belief and law, like the laws against murder both professors cite. Plaintiffs showed, rather, that there was little, if any, clearly secular advocacy against abortion at all. It is precisely what Schauer admonishes against.

Yet it seems inconceivable that the plaintiffs could win. No social issue, whose resolution has implications far beyond religious doctrine or values, can be roped off from political advocacy, regardless of its source. While we hardly wish to see political debate become a religious battle, the solution cannot be to make believe that religious values do not color discussion of public issues.

The Supreme Court rejected plaintiffs' argument with only the most offhand discussion. The short shrift it received was underscored by the fact that none of the dissenters on the sharply divided court even bothered to discuss the argument.

The lesson of *McRae* seems to be that the establishment clause does not prevent religious values from influencing public discussion of values. Only when a particular sectarian viewpoint—or a number of them—is specifically sanctioned by the coercive power of the state does an establishment clause violation occur. Another way of saying this is that we are not likely to see many cases like *Epperson*. This does not mean that religious groups should or will be able to control the curriculum in schools; lines must still be drawn. But neither can it mean that their viewpoint will or can effectively be totally excluded. There is much more room for religion in public life than either Rice or Schauer acknowledge. It may sneak in by the back door, but it is there, and the courts, looking the other way, let in in. The very confusion in the jurisprudence of the establishment clause—try figuring out sometime exactly what aid to parochial schools is permitted and why—confirms this. Religion will survive even when it is—necessarily—formally excluded from our institutions and our schools.

The Menace of Moral Majority
by R. G. Puckett

The Rev. R. G. Puckett, a Baptist minister with a conservative background, holds to a view of church-state relations and
contemporary politics which is diametrically opposed to the view
espoused by the spokesmen of Moral Majority. In his essay, "The
Menace of Moral Majority," he minces no words in scoring
religious fundamentalists in general and the Rev. Jerry Falwell in
particular. At the heart of his criticism are what Puckett
describes as "Seven Fatal Flaws" in the Moral Majority approach.

Puckett offers the reader an alternative to the viewpoint of
Moral Majority which is based upon soul-liberty, local church
autonomy, and separation of church and state. He concludes with
a comment on pluralism and a statement which recognizes that
within their respective spheres both church and state are vital
institutions.

Proponents of Moral Majority believe that they are the last great hope for America. Opponents believe that Moral Majority is neither moral nor a majority. I am among the opponents!

<h1 style="text-align:center">I</h1>

There can be no clear understanding of Moral Majority without the recognition that it is a skillful blend of far right politics and far right religion commonly known as fundamentalism. The "New Right," as this hybrid movement is called, has married God-talk and flag-waving, piousness and patriotism, the Bible and public policy.

In some ways it has been a "shotgun wedding." The far-right politicians needed a device to capture the machinery of government. The far-right religionists saw the country going to hell in a handbasket, and since the proclamation of the gospel had not been as effective as they wished, whether in the institutional church or in the electronic church, a coalition with the far-right politicians gave opportunity to impose through government what had not been accomplished through the gospel. Jerry Falwell, the founder of Moral Majority, would deny this; Richard Viguerie, the fundraising genius for conservative causes, admitted it in the fall of 1980 at the National Press Club in Washington.

Falwell sees himself as God's appointed savior for America. Viguerie, along with Howard Phillips, Ed McAteer, and Paul Weyrich, see Falwell and his type as a useful device for capturing the White House, Congress, and any lesser offices that might be swept up in the tide of public reaction, resentment, and fear in a troubled era.

Fundamentalist theology was systemized in the early part of the twentieth century. The major points of fundamentalism are rooted in belief in an inerrant and infallible Bible. It is a system based on simplistic answers to complex problems with a proof-text from the Bible for every situation. While proclaiming a gospel of love and redemption, fundamentalism is actually highly legalistic and noncompassionate. It lays down the letter of the law more than the spirit of the law, and it has no patience or tolerance for those who stray from the guidelines or disagree with the rules. Fundamentalism demands total adherence or ultimate exclusion. There is no middle stance.

James Dunn, executive director of the Baptist Joint Committee on Public Affairs, calls the New Right "Gnostic Dualism." According to Dunn, for the New Right "to claim to articulate the Christian position on such a range of subjects political, social and economic is to sin presumptuously. To make such claims while clinging to an ancient heresy is amazing. To have snowed and intimidated so many, for so long, is unbelievable."

The "spirit" of fundamentalism must be noted. The issue is not merely a matter of stated beliefs but also one of style, action, and attitude. It is a mindset or a temperament, a kind of arrogance and zeal which prides itself on being God's indispensable agent to save the world. To the fundamentalists, their perspective is the theological, ethical, and moral norm for all mankind. If one does not fit their mold, he (or she) is not one of God's own!

This Protestant evangelical fundamentalism finds kindred spirits in every religion of the world—from Roman Catholicism as embodied in the pope to the Islamic faith embodied in the Ayatollah Khomeini. I cite these two as illustrations, not to be critical of them, but to point up the spirit of Protestant fundamentalism which historically would never identify with either.

Orthodoxy is indispensable to fundamentalism. Those who differ are "modernists" or "liberals." Fundamentalists try to outdo one another in being more orthodox than the other. Jerry Falwell is reported to have boasted: "Wherever you are, I'm probably right of you. If I'm not, tell me, and I'll move."

Falwell is joined in this posture by other television religion celebrities such as Pat Robertson, Jim Bakker, James Robison, and Bill Bright of Campus Crusade (who says America is being visited by plagues, because of the U.S. Supreme Court decisions on prescribed prayer and Bible reading in public schools, just as the Egyptians were plagued because they would not let the Israelites go). These persons compete with each other for the dollars which flow to the electronic church, but they find a common ground in opposing abortion, the ERA, gay rights, sex education in public schools, drugs, pornography, trashy television, SALT II, the Department of Education, defense spending cuts, the Panama Canal Treaty, and improved relations with China.

These men and others tie their political-moral concerns to a call for revival in America. Jerry Falwell may produce a TV special entitled "America, You're Too Young to Die," but one searches in vain for any substantive discussion of the Biblical, theological, or ethical rationale behind the positions advocated. "They are authoritative, dogmatic and moralistic, but hardly given to theological discourse. They give no hard facts or reasoned analysis but dogmatic denunciations of what is wrong," according to Paul Simmons, a professor of Christian ethics.

II

Let it be understood clearly that many share some of the concerns of Moral Majority. Abortion is a grave, moral matter. Drugs which destroy young lives and pornography which poisons young minds are evils to be faced. Television filth is not only degrading and a waste of time and energy, it is an embarrassing index to the level of our society—but someone must like it; it could not survive otherwise.

Let it also be understood that I believe in the Bible. Jerry Falwell has no monopoly on the Bible. My Baptist heritage is as conservative and orthodox as his, with three apparent differences: I believe in soul-liberty, local church autonomy, and separation of church and state. The last mentioned does not mean God is divorced from the country, but it does mean no brand of theology is imposed on all the citizens through the Constitution, Congress, or the Oval Office.

Authentic religious believers should participate in the political process. There is no Biblical prohibition against good citizenship. Quite the contrary. The Bible admonishes believers in God to be supporters of the state.

The pulpits of America's churches should be prophetic. The ministers who stand each week behind the "sacred desk" should bring a "word from the Lord" if they have any legitimate message or authentic ministry. Woe unto the man who claims a call from God but does not speak with the confidence of "Thus saith the Lord." Anything less than the clear sound of the trumpet will not marshall the spiritual troops for the battle with ideologies and lifestyles which destroy our society.

The congregations of America should take seriously the responsibility to educate and inform, to create an awareness and concern for the direction society is taking. The community of believers, locally and universally, should be concerned more with the spiritual welfare of mankind than they are with budgets, buildings, ecclesiastical machinery, and worldly political power. The ultimate concern of the Almighty has to be the welfare of His creation. Otherwise, He is stripped of any moral and compassionate dimension, which is something even the minimal believer in God is unwilling to concede. If religious organizations or institutions are to be regarded as earthly extensions of the divine being and purpose, then they must demonstrate the qualities of the God they purport to represent.

There are many grave questions facing our nation and the world. They deserve legitimate answers and corresponding applications of ethical values which surely may be rooted in the religious beliefs of individuals who participate in the process of the corporate society. But we cannot change society by legally imposed sectarian values.

III

In July 1981, Dr. Jerry Falwell preached a series of sermons which he entitled "The Seven Principles Which Made America Great." Consider, please, "Seven Fatal Flaws" in the approach of Falwell and his Moral Majority.

1. *Erroneous Biblical interpretation.* Despite his strong claim to belief in Biblical inerrancy, an apparent equation of the written word of God (the Bible) with the Living Word of God (Jesus, the Christ) and plenary verbal inspiration of the Scriptures, Falwell and his kind bend Biblical truth to fit their positions. Portions are ignored, other passages are taken out of context. This style of Biblical interpretation destroys the unity and totality of the message of the Bible. To quote an Old Testament passage and call it the "Judeo" ethic and to quote a New Testament passage and call it the "Christian" ethic, and then hyphenate the two as proof-texts for the Judeo-Christian ethic is not only poor scholarship, it is a simplistic system which emasculates the true meaning of the whole Bible!

2. *Inconsistencies.* Vested interests of Moral Majority over-shadow objectivity based on fact. When speaking of abortion, Falwell says America is (was) great because historically we have honored the dignity and worth of human life. He easily slides over the slavery question with a passing reference. He advocates strong military programs with an indifference to the fact that war is killing. Welfare programs are regarded as the natural out-growth of corrupt, excessive bureaucratic government, but little concern is demonstrated for hunger, poverty, and the dehuman-ization of millions.

Morality is put on a pedestal but credibility is put in the gutter. Something is drastically wrong when a television preacher intentionally misrepresents a conversation with the President of the United States and then lightly dismisses the fact with a half-hearted apology that it was "reckless" speech. In 1981, Falwell declared he would never drape the cross with an American flag, but the jacket of his booklet on the "I Love America" rallies features a cross draped in a well-worn American flag.

3. *False equations.* Simplistic theology and politics have been equated to a frightening degree. Is God concerned about the Department of Education, the Panama Canal treaty, or our ties with Taiwan, more than He is concerned with the IRS, the Helsinki agreement, or our ties with China, the most populous country on the face of the earth?

In citing Old Testament concepts of the political order and its relationship to God, Falwell fails to recognize that ancient Israel was a theocracy; modern Israel is not. To equate the United States with ancient Israel is an outrageous application of the Bible, history, and political reality.

4. *Blurring tax categories.* A serious technical, legal, ethical, and hence moral, abuse is the crossing of clear tax classification boundaries. Political action groups are by IRS definition 501(c) (4) entities, which means that they are tax-exempt, but that contributions to the organizations are not tax-deductible for the donors. Religious organizations are classified 501(c) (3) which means they are tax-exempt and contributions can be deducted by the donors. If one is to be highly moral and ethical, the pulpit cannot be used to endorse candidates or lobby for particular legislation. Falwell played games with words and endorsed Ronald Reagan for president. He is clear in his pulpit advocacy for a constitutional amendment prohibiting abortion, the Helms proposals to get required religious activities into public schools, and legislation for tuition tax credits for private schools. The conduct of Falwell clearly raises questions about the Thomas Road Baptist Church of Lynchburg and the "Old-Time Gospel Hour," and whether they should continue to enjoy the benefits of the 501(c) (3) tax status.

Falwell's political activity is similar to that of the orthodox Roman Catholic Church hierarchy so visible in the 1940s and 1950s and to some degree now, or some of the liberal Protestant ecumenists of the 1960s and 1970s. It should be understood clearly that there is little difference in these three groups as to their efforts to impose their theological positions on all citizens through political activity. It appears each has learned from the others!

5. *Hit-list tactics.* Moral Majority insists it does not endorse candidates. Perhaps! But there is no question about the disendorsement of certain candidates, usually over single issues. Smear campaigns, hate literature, and door-to-door politicking are techniques which can be documented as devices used by Moral Majority affiliates in different areas of the country during the elections of 1980. A good example is the case of John Buchanan, an eight-term member of Congress from the Birmingham, Alabama, area until his defeat by a candidate supported by Moral Majority. His classic comment was, "Moral Majority beat my brains out with Christian love."

6. *Mandatory agreement of political positions and Christian authenticity.* Moral Majority and its spokesmen, such as Jerry Falwell, have assumed the attitude that if someone differs with them on a given political position, that person is not a genuine Christian. That attitude is arrogant, judgmental, and un-Christian. There are Christians who hold positions on political issues but there is no "Christian position" on a given issue. The kind of "absolutism" which provides no freedom for differing conscientious positions on major issues is a contradiction of the

Biblical concept of grace. It is a new form of religious legalism which Christ and the New Testament church leaders strongly denounced.

7. *Exploitation of fear and resentment.* There can be little dispute about the presence of some critical issues in American life. Many persons are genuinely concerned about conditions and trends. Any thoughtful and informed person can raise legitimate questions.

The supreme question is, "What do we do about these matters?" Certainly commitment to the best interests of individuals and the nation demands that we act with integrity and compassion. In the process, we must not deliberately distort facts, cloud issues, and exploit the fear and resentment of persons who are genuinely concerned or misunderstand the situation. Fears and prejudices should not be tools to mobilize persons to act hastily and unwisely. Polarization should be avoided where possible and inflammatory "power" words should not incite overreaction. Rhetoric, used without regard for accuracy, fairness, and justice, is in itself a serious moral issue.

IV

America is a pluralistic nation. It has been from the beginning and becomes more so with each passing decade. In a democratic society which rightfully takes seriously its responsibility to all citizens, the rights and privileges of all must be considered, even of the smallest minorities. History will judge any civilization not by how much power it had so much as by how it used that power; not by how the majority fared as by how its least influential citizens were treated. No small religious group, even one with a self-proclaimed "divine mandate," can be allowed to impose its theology on the whole nation.

Church and state are not mutually exclusive institutions. Mankind needs both. Each should make its contribution to the total well-being of all the citizens in its respective area. In areas of common concern, church and state need not be competitive, with each trying to control the other, and each need not use the structures and resources of the other to accomplish its own goals.

Jesus said, "Render therefore unto Caesar the things which be Caesar's, and unto God the things which be God's."

The U.S. Supreme Court stated in the *Everson* decision: "We have staked our very existence as a nation and as a people on the belief that separation of church and state is good for the church and good for the state."

For different reasons, I respect and accept these two statements. I wholeheartedly agree with both.

Speaking for Moral Majority
by Cal Thomas

In his essay, "Speaking for Moral Majority," Cal Thomas energetically defends the right, and indeed the duty, of conservative Christians to advance what he sees as their moral agenda. He distinguishes between separation of church and state, with which he claims to agree, and separation of church "from" state, maintaining that the Founding Fathers never intended the establishment clause to be interpreted so as to separate the one from the other. He is critical of the courts and, to some degree, the press. He also calls attention to the fact that liberal clergy have often engaged in politics in the past in order to advance their own particular agenda, as in the case of anti-war or civil rights activists. On that score, he insists that clergy such as the Rev. Jerry Falwell have the same citizen rights. Thomas addresses some of the criticisms directed at Moral Majority and explains the planks in the organization's platform. Perhaps the most telling point that Thomas makes is that the central issue is not whether some moral code will be instituted, because one will; the issue is whose moral code it is to be.

I am not a theologian. To say that is neither to brag nor complain. Until recently I had never even walked on the grounds of a seminary. I am simply a layman who happens to be a follower, and a poor one at that, of Jesus Christ. My background has been in broadcast journalism, in a career that has spanned twenty-one years and included time at NBC News in Washington, and work at an NBC affiliate in Houston, Texas, in public television, and in numerous other assignments.

I came to Moral Majority in August 1980, because I felt the country was in grave danger from moral erosion; that America had slid off the moral and spiritual underpinnings that had sustained her for 205 years. As a Christian, I know that I will someday have to give an account of my life before the infinite, personal God. I also know that if I see poverty, either physical or spiritual, and do nothing to alleviate that poverty, I am an accessory to a crime, as much as one who drives the getaway car for some bank robbers. The driver did not hold the gun on the teller, but he was an accessory in the eyes of the law.

In any case, the issue before us has more to do with rights and responsibilities than it does theology. Some time ago at the National Prayer Breakfast in Washington, the late Bishop Fulton J. Sheen spoke eloquently about our seemingly unquenchable lust for rights in America. Everyone is after his or her rights. No one, he said, is talking about his or her responsibilities. Said Bishop Sheen, "There is no freedom given without an accompanying responsibility."

John F. Kennedy said much the same thing in his inaugural address some twenty years ago. Said Kennedy, "Ask not what your country can do for you. Ask what you can do for your country."

I have asked what I can do for my country and I believe that God has led me to work at Moral Majority. Now let me say something, with my limited theological background, about the call of God.

We know from reading the Bible that not every Christian, for example, is called to teach or evangelize or preach. If I am called of God to be a missionary to Africa, however, does that mean I am anti-South America? Of course not.

I believe God has called Senator Mark Hatfield of Oregon, a liberal Republican, and Senator Sam Nunn of Georgia, a conservative Democrat, to the Senate of the United States. They often disagree on political matters, but they meet at least weekly for prayer and fellowship. Is one of them out of God's will when they disagree on a particular issue? Of course not. In fact, both may be in God's will. I believe that God has appointed checks and balances in the church as we have appointed checks and balances in our government.

There has been a trend in America for several decades to secularize government in the same way we use bleach to remove all dirt from clothing. There are those who wish to "bleach" the culture free of any religious influence whatsoever, unless they can use religion and religious people to advance their agenda. I need not tell you of recent presidents who have used religion and religious leaders to influence the minds and hearts of the people. But it is impossible to bleach America of her religious roots. Indeed, religious values and principles, and most especially Judeo-Christian values and principles, are at the heart of our government and our culture.

Thomas Jefferson, though a deist, understood well the need for certain basic rights to be unalienable—out of the reach of the institutions of men and women. What makes an unalienable right? Why, the fact that it is endowed by the Creator, of course. Any right that is not so endowed is not unalienable and may be abridged by the legislature, the courts, or by executive order.

Today, religion and religious principles are suffering from discrimination of the worst kind. Today, what Os Guiness has called "privatized religion" is very popular in our culture. "Privatized religion" means that you may hold to your personal religious views, but you must never, never try to implement into public law any views based on that value system. To do that is deemed anti-pluralistic. That is forcing one view on other people. That is, we are told, imposing a specific moral viewpoint.

I remember when President Carter went to South Korea to meet with the late President Park Chung Hee. I was a member of the president's Sunday School class at First Baptist Church in Washington. He shared with us a meeting he had had with President Park during which Mr. Carter expressed his faith in Jesus Christ.

The New York Times published a ridiculous editorial criticizing Mr. Carter for sharing his faith. The editorial said that the president had violated the separation of church and state and that by telling President Park about Christ, he had implied that Buddhism, the faith of President Park, was an inferior religion.

I wrote a letter to the editor, which the Times published, in which I pointed out that Mr. Carter was being true to his faith and to the great commission in which Jesus Christ urged his followers to go into all the world and preach the Gospel. I said the president was correct in what he did and, in fact, might have been in for some criticism had he seen an opportunity to share his faith and failed to do so.

What were the intentions of the Founding Fathers when they wrote the First Amendment? Some people are surprised to learn that the phrase "God helps those who help themselves" is not in the Bible. They are also surprised to learn that the phrase

81

"separation of church and state" appears nowhere in the Constitution. Let us be aware that the First Amendment says this: "Congress shall make no law respecting an establishment of religion, or prohibiting the free exercise thereof; or abridging the freedom of speech, or of the press, or the right of the people to assemble, and petition the government for a redress of grievances."

We believe in the concept of separation of church and state. Certainly Jefferson did, as well, though the phrase was avoided in the Constitution. Writing to a group of Virginia Baptists a few years after the Constitution was ratified, Jefferson articulated the concept of separation of church and state. But nowhere in any document I have been able to find did the Founding Fathers advocate separation of church *from* state. In fact, it was Franklin (hardly a right-wing fundamentalist), who suggested prayer as the glue that would bind the colonies together at the First Continental Congress, and who forged, through prayer, the United (and not divided) States.

In the Soviet Union we have the best example of separation of church *from* state. The church is allowed to have influence only in those areas where the state has no interest. Since the Soviet government expresses an interest in everything, the influence of the church is confined to its own four walls and then only if it cooperates with the government and is not viewed as a threat.

Writing for the American Enterprise Institute, the scholar Michael Malbin has done a marvelous study of the intentions of the authors of the First Amendment and compared those intentions with modern court decisions. In his monograph, Malbin notes that the Supreme Court has held since 1947 that the establishment clause requires both Congress and the states to maintain strict neutrality between religion and irreligion in any laws that might conceivably aid private religious organizations. Legal disputes since then have had to do with the differences between "aid" to religion which is prohibited, neutrality which is required, and hostility which supposedly is prohibited. Free exercise legal doctrine, in contrast, has been anything but neutral. Says Malbin, "As the court has espoused its doctrines, it has relied on an incredibly flawed reading of the intentions of the authors of the First Amendment. Unfortunately, modern scholars are little better. Some are good on isolated points, but rarely has one tried to explain the complexities of the establishment issue or the relationship between establishment and free exercise." He adds, "Precisely what was meant when the people were granted the right to exercise their religion freely needs detailed exploration. It is clear, however, that it did not mean what modern judges claim."

Malbin goes on to fill some of the scholarly vacuum and cites

Thomas Lloyd's shorthand notes compiled in *The Annals of Congress*. The *Annals* were the forerunner of today's *Congressional Record* and they record the debates involving James Madison, Peter Sylvester, and other members of that first body as they sought to forge what we now call the First Amendment. The logic and the give and take on this issue are quite revealing. I commend Malbin's monograph.

Next, let me deal briefly with the most commonly raised objections to Moral Majority. Liberal preachers, after first denouncing our right to speak, were quickly brought up short on the hypocritical scale when it was pointed out that they exercised their right to speak out on political and social issues during the 1960s and 1970s. Caught in that trap, they retreated and attempted to hold a new position. That position is, basically, that they are right in the way they approach issues, but we are wrong. But, they proceed from a non-absolute base; that is, that the Bible is full of errors and that each of us must select what fits in with his or her worldview and lifestyle and reject the rest as culturally derived folklore.

Having established a philosophical beachhead on shifting sand, these liberals then go on to say that we have no right to impose our particular views on everybody else. We are perfectly free to practice what we believe to be true in our own personal lives, but we have no right to try to pass laws or keep other laws from being passed that "force" people to conform to those views. Let us examine that logic and see why it is flawed. It will not take long!

I have been reading about the Dred Scott decision. In 1857, the Supreme Court, using the type of logic I just described, said that blacks were not fully human and, therefore, whites were entitled to own them as property. This, said the court, was not the imposition of a moral viewpoint, because no one was forced to own a slave. Those who wished to own slaves might do so. Those for whom slavery was morally or religiously objectionable did not have to own slaves. The vote was 7 to 2. By that margin and by that logic, the Supreme Court in 1973 approved abortion on demand.

During the Vietnam War I was often tear-gassed as I covered the anti-war demonstrations for NBC News. I remember well the liberal harangues about the immorality of the Vietnam War. I remember William Sloan Coffin and the Berrigan brothers who urged kids to go to Canada and break the law. The Berrigans and their followers broke into draft board offices and poured blood on selective service records. I remember those, within the church and without, who said you were immoral if you supported the immoral Vietnam War. Boycotts were conducted against Dow Chemical's bathroom cleaner and their other products because

Dow manufactured napalm, which was used in bombs for that immoral war.

During the civil rights movement of the 1960s, it was the preachers who provided the moral impetus that resulted in civil rights legislation. Americans were forced to do battle with their consciences and with racism in their own hearts because of the moral arguments against racism articulated so well by Dr. Martin Luther King and many others.

Today we have laws against stealing, murder, rape, incest, and cannibalism. I am sure there are thieves, people who would like to murder, practitioners of rape and incest, and a minority who would like to eat their neighbors, who feel that their "rights" have been abridged because somebody else's moral values have been imposed on them, preventing them from carrying out their desires or, at least, imposing heavy penalties upon them if they do.

The fact is that *all* law is the imposition of someone's morality over someone else's morality. The question is not whether one form of morality will be imposed over another form. The question is, which form and whose morality? The answer is whichever has the best track record and best likelihood for success. We believe that the morality that comes from the Judeo-Christian value base has the best track record and provides the best foundation for an orderly society. All laws come from the Judeo-Christian value base.

Another criticism of Moral Majority is that we sometimes appear arrogant. If standing on principles and setting forth our view of right and wrong seems arrogant, okay, we are arrogant. But I would rather be arrogantly right than wishy-washy, and for the sake of what some call "pluralism" not take a stand for anything simply because I might offend someone or because someone might disagree with me.

I was once called arrogant by William Sloan Coffin during a debate at Florida State University. When I stepped to the microphone and recalled that I had covered Coffin's anti-war speeches during the Vietnam War era and that, as I recalled, nobody was more arrogant and sure of the righteousness of his cause than Bill Coffin, he sort of half-smiled. Then a student in the audience, the one I think who came dressed as a witch as a commentary on Moral Majority, screamed as loud as he could, "Yeah, and he was right, too." I think the student made my point better than I could have made it. So, one man's arrogance is another man's steadfastness.

What is Moral Majority really all about and what are we trying to do? Recall, if you will, the movie *Network*. The star of the film was a television network news anchorman. During a particularly exciting scene, the newsman said to his audience,

"Now I want all of you to get up out of your seats right now and go to your windows. I want you to open your windows, lean out and yell as loud as you can, 'I'm mad as hell and I'm not going to take it anymore.'" If we could get away with it, we would probably use that as our slogan!

Many hundreds of thousands of people who have joined Moral Majority and many others who have not established a formal relationship with us but who do agree with our issues and the stands we take, are "mad as hell and are not going to take it anymore." These are the people who have seen the values and views that are dear to them trampled underfoot by secular humanists and other liberals who, they believe, have turned freedom into license and tolerance for diversity into a green light for anything.

Many of our people have been the turned-off voters. They have believed that it does not matter who is elected because all politicians are crooks. They have believed their votes do not matter. So, they have not voted.

But in the 1980 election, we were able to mobilize and motivate millions of previously turned-off and inactive voters to go to the polls by asking them to consider an agenda of moral issues. We did not suggest that these are the only moral issues or that if anyone disagrees with us, they are, by definition, relegated to an immoral minority. That view is a creation of the press.

Of course, our issues were not solely responsible for producing the results of 1980. The fact that the economy was a mess, that Americans were being held hostage in Iran and the rescue effort had failed, that our defense capabilities were a serious concern, that Soviet troops were in Afghanistan and threatening Poland, and that Cuba, Russia's puppet, was helping to undermine the peace in El Salvador and in Africa, all combined with the issues we raised to bring about change. But our issues were and are the gut issues that our people believe most directly and most immediately affect their lives and values and even the future of the country.

What are those issues? You have probably heard that we have positions on everything from the 55 m.p.h. speed limit to the movie *The Empire Strikes Back!*

Briefly, we stand for four basic issues. First, we are pro-life, and that includes not only unborn human life but so-called handicapped life (and we are all handicapped by sin), rich life, poor life, black life, white life. We believe the burden of proof is on the pro-abortionist to prove that human life does *not* begin at conception. This has been believed medically and biologically as well as theologically, at least in the Judeo-Christian tradition, throughout much of history. Only since the erosion of the authority of Scripture, and of authority in general, has a different view been not only accepted but also evangelized.

Second, we favor and support the traditional family, the husband-wife relationship. To support the traditional family does not mean we necessarily think that women ought to stay at home. It means only the male-female relationship. We oppose legislation that would grant to homosexual "marriages" the status of family for the sake of tax and other laws. We oppose special civil rights for homosexuals because theirs is a chosen lifestyle and they are not a legitimate minority. I have talked to many people who have come out of homosexuality. I have never talked to a person who has come out of blackness. We believe the traditional family is the foundation for any free and strong nation or society.

Third, we are pro-moral. Under this broad umbrella come two sub-tenets. One is our opposition to the spread of pornography, which we believe is mind-pollution. We have an Environmental Protection Agency to watch the quality of air we breathe and water we drink. I am not suggesting a federal pornography agency, but pollution of the mind and spirit can be just as damaging, if not more so, than air and water pollution. The second pro-moral tenet is our opposition to the legalization of illegal drugs. We believe that the drug culture is a new form of slavery.

Fourth, and finally, we are pro-American, not chauvinistically so, but lovingly so. Therefore, in order to preserve our freedoms and way of life and hold out the lamp of freedom to the world, we favor a strong national defense. That is not because we believe ultimate security is in missiles. It is not. But, in a fallen and imperfect world, there are those who would seek to deprive us even of the right to agree and disagree. We must, therefore, be stronger than those who would eliminate those freedoms.

We also support the nation of Israel. That does not mean we support Israel on every policy decision. It does mean that we stand by Israel's right to exist and recognize the need for a homeland for the Jewish people so that there will never again be a holocaust. We remember how even President Roosevelt refused admission to the Jews when they fled from Nazi exterminators. That must never happen again.

The only people who would not try to assert or "impose" their views in public law are those who do not believe that those views are true. If you believe abortion is the taking of innocent human life, would you not be a hypocrite of hypocrites if you failed to act on that belief? Members of the "I am personally opposed, but..." Club make me sick. Can you imagine what the reaction would be if someone said, "I am personally opposed to discrimination, but I am not going to vote for civil rights laws because that would impose my moral viewpoint on bigots who wish to discriminate"?

It is a philosophically untenable position. One must ask, "What in the world makes you personally opposed?"

Finally, let me address the question of historical religious involvement in America. The First Amendment prohibits the government from establishing a church (as had been done in England). It does not prevent the churches from doing anything, except collecting taxes. Any person who suggests that separation of church and state requires more than this (that it requires churches to remain silent on so-called "political issues" or requires preachers to be neutral on candidates—which we are, by the way—or requires religious organizations to pursue only "spiritual goals") is simply grinding his own axe rather than reading the law.

It was the preachers and those they led who changed our monarchy into a republic. And what became of it? A clerical tyranny? A crackpot theocracy? Or a new birth of freedom?

Many contemporary preachers, and Jerry Falwell has taken the blame for this as much as anyone, have in the past led church people not into action, but into inaction. The result has been an abdication of moral leadership in the nation to individuals and to forces who would impose the tyranny of immorality.

There was none of the editorial posturing we read today during the 1960s or 1970s about liberal clergymen speaking out on political issues. I recall no editorials or denunciations against President Johnson for calling Martin Luther King, Andy Young, Billy Graham, or Cardinal Cook and, occasionally, having them to dinner and asking them to spend the night at the White House. But let Jerry Falwell receive one call from Ronald Reagan and the republic is in danger. Let him get a call from Menachem Begin and you would think a crime had been committed.

New York's liberal Democratic Senator Daniel Moynihan said recently on "Good Morning America," "We are a blessed people, but we are not elect and we must shape our future as we have our past or we risk losing our freedoms." I can think of no better statement concerning the purpose of Moral Majority.

On the front of the National Archives building in Washington, D.C., there is an inscription from Shakespeare that says, "What is past is prologue." The values and traditions that built America were the prologue to the economic, political, and spiritual prosperity that followed.

There is something that is worse than war and worse, even, than speaking out. It is silence! The grossest immoralities have been perpetrated not by those who carried them out, but by those who remained silent and did nothing. We may not always be right, but we will never be judged guilty of saying and doing nothing.

Theological Dimensions of
Church-State Relations
by David Little

Commenting on the essays of Cal Thomas and the Rev. R. G. Puckett, David Little sees the key issues between the two as being *"the legislation of public morality and the relation of religious belief and affirmation to that question." His own essay, entitled "Theological Dimensions of Church-State Relations," explores the free-church tradition, to which he himself subscribes, by discussing the contributions of Roger Williams to that tradition.*

Little also devotes some attention to the differences between the free-church model and the revivalist model in our religious history. In this context, he touches upon such contemporary issues as the so-called "electronic church" and "televangelism," focusing in particular upon the ministry of the Rev. Jerry Falwell.

It has recently been alleged that, thanks to the rise of the electronic church or "televangelists," as they are called, we are in the midst of a new religious reformation, parallel in many important ways to the Protestant Reformation of the sixteenth century. As James A. Taylor has said:

> Our churches today find themselves in a situation similar to that of the Roman Catholic Church at the time of the Protestant Reformation. A new expression of religion has come on the scene, and we don't know what to make of it. Five hundred years ago, Rome attacked the Reformation with the Inquisition. Or it attempted to ignore it, with excommunication. But the Reformation wouldn't go away, and neither will the new evangelism—because the technologies that spawned each of the movements won't go away.
> The Reformation could not have happened without the invention of printing, which put the Scriptures into the hands of the laity....Put another way, the Reformation was the child of printing....In much the same way, evangelicalism today is a child of television....

What shall we make of this claim? Are we really experiencing a phenomenon as significant for us in theological, political, economic, and social terms as the Reformation was for Europe and eventually for the whole Anglo-Saxon world?

Surely not. The Protestant Reformation was associated with cultural, social, and political changes—the rise of nationalism and secularization, the emergence of constitutional government and religious pluralism, the "elevation of the laity," and so on— that in scope and extent are not equivalent to anything we are presently experiencing, television or no television.

Nevertheless, there may be something of interest about this way of contrasting the Reformation and the present in relation to the kind of technology that accompanies each period. It is true that the technology of printing was indispensable to the spread of the Protestant Reformation. It is also true that the capacity to disseminate the written word complemented the content and emphasis of the Reformation message. People were not only able—as the result of printing—to read the Word of God for themselves; they could also study it, and, in addition, study other words that bore upon the Bible. Moreover, those affected by the Reformation were prompted to organize themselves so that having studied their Bibles, they might better enrich, and, if necessary, correct one another. In short, the advent of printing both reinforced and helped to implement Luther's famous Reformation slogan, "the priesthood of all believers."

Further on, I want to contrast rather sharply the connection of printing and the Reformation with the connection of the electronic media and some aspects of contemporary religious life. But first, I wish to draw attention to some of the effects of the Reformation upon our own American religious life, particularly as that teaching was mediated through the influence of left-wing Puritan groups in seventeenth-century England, some of which were directly represented in Colonial America by people like Roger Williams, the Quakers, and others. Interestingly, the proliferation of these groups in England and later in America was in many ways the result of the profusion of pamphlets, tracts, and sermons made possible by the medium of printing.

These left-wing religious groups gave the idea of the priesthood of all believers a radical twist, in two ways. 1) For them, religious life was fundamentally active participation in small democratic fellowship. As the distinguished English social theorist, A. D. Lindsay, puts it:

> Perhaps the most significant thing about Puritan democratic theory is that the Puritans began with the experience of working in a small and thoroughly democratic society, the Puritan congregation. Their idea of a church is that it is a fellowship of active believers. The Puritans of the Left, with whom democratic theories mostly originated, were all congregationalists—to use the late term. The self-governing congregation was for them the church. In such a society all are equal, in the sense, as we have seen, that they were all equally called of God...and therefore all equally called on to contribute to the common discussion about the purpose and actions of their small society. Their genuine experienced democracy was not political, but the democracy of a voluntary society—a society which did not use force in putting into practice its decisions, but was a *fellowship of discussion.* (Italics added)

2) There was a strong emphasis, for example in the thought of Roger Williams, upon a universal right to freedom of conscience. Two important implications of this doctrine are worth stressing. First, each individual believer is understood to be free to

determine and follow his or her own religious (or non-religious) convictions without civil coercion or control. Said Williams:

> In vain have English Parliaments permitted English Bibles in the poorest English houses, and the simplest man or woman to search the Scriptures, if yet against their soul's persuasion from the Scripture, they should be forced...to believe as the Church believes. [And, as one commentator, Edmund S. Morgan, goes on: For Williams] England and New England needed all the light they could get from the simplest man or woman who read them as well as from the most learned minister....

Rather than employing civil coercion, persuasion alone must be used in religious affairs. Even scriptural truth is won only by search and trial, by "chewing and rational weighing and consideration," in Williams' unforgettable words. Second, and in accordance with his commitment to the sovereignty of each and every conscience, Williams drove a very large wedge between church and state.

> Now there being two states, the civil or corporeal and the ecclesiastical or spiritual, there are consequently two sorts of laws, two sorts of transgressions, two sorts of punishments, to wit, civil and spiritual....

The "spiritual sword" and the "sword of steel" are two different things, and ought under no circumstances to be confused. That they had been manifestly confused in the Massachusetts Bay Colony, from which Williams was summarily expelled, accounted, Williams believed, for the tyranny of that community and others like it. To believe that religious conviction and practice might be subjected to coercion was itself the "bloody tênent," which disrupted both church and state.

But Williams' doctrine was still more radical than this. Drawing upon a common Puritan emphasis, he distinguished sharply between the first and the second tables of the Decalogue, between special revelation and the duties and practice pertinent to that, on the one hand, and what he called "the law of nature, the law moral and civil," on the other. He explicitly and repeatedly defended the idea that the law moral and civil was natural to every human being and provided a sufficient foundation for organizing and directing civil society. Having Christians in office was decidedly *not* a necessary requirement for preserving the safety and welfare of the social order. In defending the rights of non-Christians to hold political office, Williams states:

[T]here is a moral virtue, a moral fidelity, ability, and honesty, by which other men (beside Church-members) are, by good nature and education, by good laws and good examples nourished and trained up in, that civil places need not be monopolized into the hands of Church-members (who sometimes are not fitted for them), and all others deprived of their natural and civil rights and liberties.

Williams' doctrine of the separation of church and state, then, presupposed an important distinction between religious and moral truth. He clearly and self-consciously advocated a *secular* state whose peace and order could be maintained only by reference to an autonomous law of nature or reason. Moreover, this law must be observed for the health *both* of religion *and* of civil society.

In short, a commitment to the principle of freedom of conscience, such as Williams recommended, rests upon a shared belief that civil or public morality is indeed determinable independently of appeals of particular religious beliefs or authorities.

I

In sketching the connection between the technology of printing and the development of the Reformation slogan, "the priesthood of all believers," I do not mean to imply anything necessary or inevitable about that connection. Obviously, printing might be and has been used to very different ends by different religious groups. Still, I do not think there is a certain "congeniality" (if I may employ a deliberately fuzzy word) between one thing and the other.

Similarly, I do not wish to suggest that there is anything fixed and finished about the connection between electronic technology and the predominant use currently being made of it by religious evangelists like Jerry Falwell. All I am holding out for is a comparable sort of "congeniality" between the thing television seems to do best, and the religious message and image of the religious life emphasized by the leading "televangelists."

Now the religious tradition in this country most readily adaptable to mass communication is not, I think, the "free-church" image I have alluded to. The emphasis on "participatory religion," including the active mutual engagement of free and equal members in conducting the church's life, together with the emphasis upon religious toleration and the secular state, is not easily conveyed to a mass audience.

On the contrary, the more suitable form is *American revivalism.* And that is, of course, the tradition that almost all of the televangelists stand in—certainly Falwell does. Notice that revivalism, far before any electronic medium was available, constituted what might be called "mass religion." Here were more or less large mass meetings conducted sporadically by itinerant evangelists who collected groups of believers or would-be believers in a temporary and impersonal relationship. The form of communication between evangelist and audience was all one-way. The messages were uncomplicated and often highly emotional, with wide and immediate appeal.

In addition, the messages frequently painted pictures of imminent national disaster and collapse as the result of spiritual and moral corruption. The recommended solution was of course simple and direct, as the revivalist's solution always is: to Christianize the nation, and to return to our allegedly uniform national religious roots. That could be done by striving "to bring the laws of society into subjection to [Christ's] control," and to establish "righteousness in every statute book, and in every provision of human legislation and human jurisprudence;...oh! this is the reign of Jesus"—to cite statements that typify the revivalist spirit of the nineteenth century. In the twentieth century, much of the agitation for Prohibition by evangelists like Billy Sunday was the direct outgrowth of this characteristic emphasis upon legislating the rule of Christ.

The central features of revivalism—mass religion; one-way communication; emotional, direct appeal; simple diagnoses and simple solutions; the use of dramatic, apocalyptic language; and so on—were, in short, all made for television. It is of course true that television, like traditional revivalism, does not necessarily make people inert and passive. It affects action in various ways—what is bought, what is said, and so on. But, interestingly enough, the medium itself, the process of communication that takes place between performer and viewer, is not dialogic. Seated before a television, one can cheer and one can boo, one can applaud and one can moan, but none of that affects in the slightest what the image on the screen does and says.

My point is that the rather natural affinity between re-vivalism and television carries with it its own interesting implications for religious life and outlook that are in some respects sharply at odds with the "free-church" model. For example, the one-way form of communication, which makes the viewer into a spectator, rather than an active partner in a "fellowship of discussion," appears to correlate directly with the way an evangelist like Jerry Falwell understands and organizes his own church in Lynchburg, Virginia. Falwell himself admits and defends what can only be described as an authoritarian form of church organization. To quote Frances Fitzgerald:

In a sermon titled 'The Day of Great Men Has Not Passed,' [Falwell] said, 'God's plan is that His flock is to be led by

93

shepherds, not run by a board or a committee.' He explained: 'God never intended for a committee nor a board of deacons nor any other group to dominate a church or control a pastor. The pastor is God's man, God's servant, God's leader. When you tie the hands of God's man, when you keep him from acting as the Holy Spirit leads him, you have murdered his initiative, you have killed his spirit.'

In the second place, it leads to a rather appalling understanding of what discussion is all about, as illustrated by the following news story from the January 1, 1980, *Richmond Times-Dispatch:*

From the frontier of the electronic church comes this peek into the 1980s. . . . The Rev. Jerry Falwell had been talking about the ability to spread the Gospel through the media and electronics. He continues: '. . . We're actually getting to a telephone situation where a secretary can dial you and say, "Mrs. Jones, I have Jerry Falwell on the line, do you have a moment?" push the button and I can talk to you and will talk to you and share spiritual things with you. And then I can stop and you'll respond and you'll talk—this is all in a computer now, things that I have put in there before that deal with all those kinds of things. Then when you finish talking I talk right back to you; I carry on from what you have actually said, and you come right back again, and *I'm asleep in bed at home.'* (The congregation erupts with laughter.) 'That computer picks up what you're saying and fishes around to see what Jerry said that was pretty close to that and throws me back in there. That's tremendous. I'll be plaguing the liberals till Jesus comes. They can shoot me today.' (More laughs.)

Finally, on the matter of freedom of conscience and drawing a firm distinction, as Roger Williams did, between the "law of Christ," and the natural law, the "law civil and moral," it is clear that an evangelist like Falwell stands much closer to the revivalist position than he does to the tradition of Roger Williams and the "free churches."

It is true that Falwell is somewhat ambivalent as to whether he wants to Christianize America by imposing "Bible-based" laws concerning the protection of the "traditional family," the status of women, homosexuality, censorship, abortion, and so on. He does stress, from time to time, that Moral Majority does not intend to legislate religious belief and practice, but simply to legislate (as the name implies) *moral* prescriptions. So long as one share's the moral sentiments of Moral Majority, one is invited to join that group, regardless of one's religious convictions.

Still, Falwell frequently does not observe this distinction. In his book, *Listen, America!*, Falwell bases his criticisms of existing laws concerning homosexuality, sexual practices, and other issues, on the Bible, and he clearly urges legislative and judicial reforms to bring the laws of the land into conformity with his interpretation of Christian Scripture. He is quite explicit about this. He urges citizens, as he says, to "evaluate the stand of [political] candidates on moral issues" on the basis of "a code of minimum moral standards dictated by the Bible."

At least when he is talking in this way—and he does quite often—Falwell is advocating that legislators enact laws based on the Bible. He would thus coerce all American citizens, regardless of their religious convictions, to act in accord with the moral standards concerning sexual practices, censorship, and the like, that are derived from *one particular religious interpretation;* namely, Falwell's and that of those who share his convictions.

II

We are, then, confronted with two very different models of Christian belief and of the relation of Christians to the state. The differences between the free-church model and the revivalist model are in the deepest sense *theological.* They go to the heart of what it means for people to be Christians, to hear and act upon the Word of God, and to relate to fellow Christians as well as to fellow non-Christians.

I emphasize that both models represent venerable traditions in the history of our nation. It would be mistaken for proponents of the free-church model to dismiss electronic revivalism as some recent and evanescent creature of television, as it would be for the new revivalists to try to characterize the free-church emphasis on a secular state and an aggressive doctrine of toleration as some new-fangled heresy produced by latter-day "secular humanists" or "amoral liberals." Indeed, I have taken pains to sketch Roger Williams' views just so as to leave no doubt about the pedigree of the free-church outlook. When we are talking of the "spiritual foundations" of our country, it is well to recall Williams and all he stood for.

Now these two models are, roughly speaking, represented by Mr. Thomas and the Rev. Puckett. Accordingly, the theological differences between them—over the doctrine of scripture, of the church, and of church-state relations—would, judging from their essays, fall into predictable patterns. At some point, all of those differences ought to be carefully taken up and thrashed out.

In terms of the church-state question, however, the key issue between Puckett and Thomas surely concerns the question of *the legislation of public morality and the relation of religious belief and affirmation to that question.*

Thomas makes an important point when he draws our attention to the necessity in any society of legislating on the basis of *some* set of moral beliefs, concerning, for example, the definition and limits of injury and harm, marital relations, the relations between the sexes, and between the races. And certainly in the minds of many citizens both inside *and* outside of Moral Majority, it is right and proper for all citizens to be concerned about and eager to find thoughtful and realistic solutions to many of the problems that Moral Majority is addressing.

I should think the Rev. Puckett would agree, though unfortunately he slips over these questions rather hastily in his essay. For example, the subject of TV censorship is not obviously settled merely by indicating, as the Rev. Puckett does, that there is a ready audience for salacious programs. Thomas rightly points out that the mere fact that some people want to do something is not in itself a decisive moral reason for letting them do it!

On the other hand, what has to be profoundly disturbing from the point of view of someone like the Rev. Puckett, who obviously stands in the free-church tradition of Roger Williams, is the interjection, in discussions of public morality, of parochial religious appeals to the Bible, such as one finds abundantly in the teachings of Jerry Falwell. For the follower of Roger Williams, it is the law, moral and civil—the natural law, which citizens are assumed to share independently of their religious commitments—that must serve as the basis for working out solutions to the problems of public morality. The implication is that we must look and listen for moral wisdom and insight concerning *legislated* morality from all quarters of the society, and not simply from one or another privileged religious perspective. Decisions concerning what it is right to coerce people to do may not be hammered out on the basis of scriptural texts or the utterances of a particular religious authority, however convinced the authority may be that he is "God's man." Rather, such decisions will have to be made on the basis of "what seems reasonable," "what seems just," from the perspective of *all* citizens. And, for the follower of Roger Williams, this will have to be done precisely in the name of protecting the freedom of the Gospel, as well as insuring full liberty of conscience to every citizen, regardless of religious commitment.

In short, it is not whether public morality is a question of concern to us all, but what the acceptable basis is for solving the problems of public morality. Here the two traditions are at loggerheads. As for me and mine, we stand with Roger Williams.

PART II

CONTEMPORARY POLITICAL PERSPECTIVES

The Christian Political Movement and the Intellectual Barbarians
by Edward E. McAteer

Edward E. McAteer, president of The Religious Roundtable, Inc., presents a platform for the Christian political movement which has emerged during the last five years. As an active lobbyist for the movement, McAteer has been highly successful in helping to organize political action groups with similar moral commitments. In the essay which follows, he strikes out at the advocates of abortion and encourages all "biblically committed" Christians to take an active role in political affairs. McAteer contends that it is ridiculous to suggest that political activism by Christians is contrary to the purposes and intentions of the American system of government. All authority and freedom comes from God. Consequently all aspects of governmental concern come under "the sphere of biblical application." McAteer categorically denies that the Christian political movement is ruthless or coercive. Moreover, it is not involved in unconstitutional advocacy and is, he maintains, gaining strength because it speaks to the values which Americans share.

Jesus of Nazareth was perceived as a political threat to the Roman tyranny which occupied the land of His birth and residence. Jesus was repudiated by His own Jewish nation and crucified under Roman law in the most tragic miscarriage of justice known to history.

The risen Christ commissioned His followers to proclaim the "Gospel"—good news of eternal life which He died to provide for all who will receive Him.

While Jesus did not lead a political movement as such, the spiritual movement which He inaugurated laid the foundation on which political freedoms would be constructed in the course of time.

The early Christians had no opportunity to exercise citizenship and voting rights as every Christian American does today. Therefore it is a mistake to conclude, as some do, that their lack of involvement in government implies that it is somehow "un-Christian" for us to participate in politics as Christians today.

Every citizen in America represents a unit of political influence by right of birth and citizenship in our free republic. Failure to exercise that influence for biblically-guided righteousness as the Christian perceives it means passive support of evil. This fact arises from the nature of the governmental system which we have inherited.

Following a millennium of spiritual darkness during which the established "church" wielded tyrannical power over the state and genuine followers of Christ were persecuted and tortured, the great reformers of the sixteenth century restored the New Testament doctrine of justification by faith. This meant that salvation was no longer dispensed by a corrupt "church." It was available, as Jesus had taught, when an individual, by free choice, received the Savior and the benefits of His atonement.

The bondage of the human spirit ended when men and women awoke to the fact that Jesus Christ is the only mediator between God and man (1 Timothy 2:5). The yoke of tyranny was broken, and history turned a corner. The spiritual liberation which began on a mass scale with the Reformation became the foundation of a new freedom movement in the civic, legal, economic, social, and governmental realms of life.

Indeed, all true freedom arises from the God-given reality of spiritual freedom in the hearts of the masses of individuals who are the building blocks of a society.

The charters of the American colonies recognized the Hand of God in bringing people to the shores of the New World for the fulfillment of His purposes. The Bible shaped the political thinking of the colonial clergymen. "Their political speeches were sermons [according to Alice M. Baldwin], their political slogans were often Bible texts. What they taught of government had about it the authority of the divine."

The Declaration of Independence recognized God as the author of freedom, and expounded the view that God is above government. The Declaration asserted that government is a creation of the people, and its purpose is to guarantee and perpetuate God-given rights.

"A Christian world and life view [says Professor C. Gregg Singer] furnished the basis of this early political thought, which guided the American people for nearly two centuries, and whose crowning lay in the writing of the Constitution of 1787."

Confidence in the Bible as the special and unique revelation of the mind and will of God to man is the basic driving force motivating the Christian citizen. In fact, no conceivable concern of government lies outside the sphere of biblical application. Three major themes running through the Bible are God's declared purposes for 1) the family, 2) the church, and 3) the nation and its government.

Morality, in the Christian understanding of the term, is rooted in the spiritual perceptions which arise from biblical understanding. The biblically-committed Christian segment of our population is a moral force precisely because it believes God has delivered to man certain truths and principles which are applicable to moral issues.

The Connecticut Mutual Life Insurance survey on American values discovered an amazing fact—the existence of some 40 million biblically-oriented citizens, just under the surface of American life, who in fact constitute a political force capable of changing the face of the nation.

At first the research analysts could not believe the survey data, and they subjected it to strenuous scientific cross-checking procedures. The very same evidence rose to the surface in every instance. The conclusion is inescapable: the biblically-guided citizen has in fact emerged as a mighty political force in American life.

Denominational walls are meaningless relics of earlier times. When it comes to changing the leadership and direction of America, evangelicals, fundamentalists, conservative Catholics, Jews, black Christians and mainline Protestants unite in a common purpose to preserve the family and to relate principles of

101

truth, freedom, equity, and justice in American life.

All elements of the Christian political movement concur in the encouragement of Christian involvement in government. In the tradition of the colonial forefathers, they unite in a common purpose to foster better government through application of perceived biblical guidelines.

The purpose of influencing public policy on moral issues is paramount—and there is a strong tendency to perceive *all* governmental issues as *moral* issues.

The Christian political movement is committed to the view that the free exercise clause of the First Amendment guarantees the right of voluntary Scripture reading and prayer in public schools and in other tax-supported institutions. Also, in the interest of academic freedom it is only right that the view that God created the universe should be presented among the various concepts of the origin of life.

While adhering to the principle that both church and state are ultimately responsible to God Almighty, the movement promotes freedom of conscience and responsible action as a service rendered to God, within the spheres of church and state.

The Christian political movement advocates a biblical view of leadership. This means that those who occupy positions of leadership should be guided by the principles of truth, love, justice, responsibility, and integrity that are reflected in the sacred pages. It means also that these very same principles which characterize the personal life of the leader must be carried into government when he or she is elected to public office. Government can be no better than those who render the decisions which shape the policies and ordinances under which a governed people must live.

Long centuries ago the great King Solomon declared a principle of government which is valid throughout all earthly time: "When the righteous are in authority, the people rejoice; but when the wicked bear rule, the people mourn" (Proverbs 29:2).

And earlier, King David had written of the tragic consequences of evil leadership in the sphere of government: "The scepter of wickedness shall not rule over the land of the righteous, lest the righteous be forced to do wrong" (Psalm 125:3).

The program of the Christian political movement also promotes a biblical view of the family. The movement is pro-family in the biblical sense. As such, it opposes abortion as an act of murder. It stands opposed to euthanasia on the same grounds. Further, it holds that parents, rather than the state, are responsible for the upbringing and education of children and youth.

The threat in our day comes not from the Christian political movement, but from the intellectual barbarians.

A concept known as "body count" has become a daily news

item. The Khmer Rouge in Cambodia intensified the slaughter of natives. Pol Pot took his place beside Lenin, Stalin, Mao, and Hitler as his planners sought "year zero" through a purposeful genocide of a whole people. Native Cambodians were trained in the mind set of the intellectual barbarians.

The twentieth century is the age of Auschwitz which was built on the corruption of the German legal and medical professions in the 1920s and 1930s. The Nazis developed the concept of life devoid of value where the state would rid itself of useless eaters. The Nazi's elite increased the death toll by more millions, and in China the supposed forces of progress deemed that a landlord class must be killed. Those in power loosely defined who was useful. Millions died.

In the midst of today's news about body count, search and destroy missions, and the tallying of death figures by a computer's sophisticated technology, the Nixon-era Supreme Court issued a ruling that Americans may kill Americans for convenience as long as it is done in the first nine months of human existence, and so long as the mother herself is willing to have the child killed. And thus in an act of murder scheduled in clinical surroundings by males in white coats with subservient nurses in attendance, the primeval bond between mother and child is shattered, and the new victim of the lethal age of the twentieth century is assaulted murderously.

The twentieth century is the century of the intellectual barbarians, the century of Auschwitz, Cambodia, and the United States Supreme Court. Who indeed are these intellectual barbarians? From where do they come? They are the alienated products of a modern society whose education has produced a thinking machine and not a thinking and feeling human being.

These intellectual barbarians have many crocodile tears and programs for humanity in general, but they have nothing for individual human beings. Simple existence means nothing to them; youth must be useful and wanted in order to live. The fact of life, the beauty of life, the reality of life, the enjoyment of life are not as important to the intellectual barbarians as is their own vanity. They perceive themselves as intelligent and sensitive in the trendy and fashionable pharisaic society which they inhabit. They wax eloquent on the furbish lousewort and the snail darter, but they accept the wholesale slaughter of a million per year of their own kind. With a straight face, these intellectual barbarians will proclaim their dedication to the poor and offer them the "modest proposal" of killing their young. (Jonathan Swift, one recalls, used satire to suggest that the starving youth of Ireland be used for food, but satire in America can offer no competition to reality.) We here in America have enacted the "modest proposal."

These intellectual barbarians proclaim their belief in racial justice, but they enact, support, and fail to protest government programs which kill black babies in genocidal proportions. They pride themselves on being opposed to discrimination against women, but they favor studies to determine the sex of a child before birth. If the child is not the sex the mother wishes, it is killed. That child feels pain, dies in pain. Statistics show that the child is usually female. To be killed by men masked in white, at a mother's request, because one is a girl, is sexism.

The pro-life movement rebukes the intellectual barbarians who comprise the liberal and conservative elites. It exposes them as deceitful and lying hypocrites who do not care for human beings or for humanity. Pro-lifers are called fanatics because they will not be silent about the reality of the child with hands and feet and heart and mind who was killed because she was inconvenient, the wrong sex, or a social embarrassment.

Where, one may well ask, are these intellectual barbarians who supposedly are concerned about the ecology of baby seal killing but super-sophisticated about killing baby human beings leading us? That's a good question. Of one thing we may be certain; when this atheistic and blatant generation has passed on and left its footprints in the shifting sands of time, Jehovah God's all powerful, ever enduring, never compromising word will with a clarion call still be sounding out the clear condemnation. Sure judgment will result for individuals and even nations. "They who do violence to the blood of any person shall flee to the pit," despite intellectual barbarians, Supreme Court justices, and approving senators.

What will we do in this destiny-deciding decade of the intellectual barbarians? The struggle is not a new battle for which we have been called to sacrifice. It is older than when the Babylonians threw their children into the fires of Baal and Mammon and Kings Ahaz and Manesseh offered child sacrifices to the pagan god Moloch in the ancient valley of Gehenna. Even now the new Babylonians and barbarians demand again the blood sacrifice. Many public figures who personally oppose the spilling of blood wash their hands as did Pilate. But the blood is like the blood on Lady Macbeth's hands; it will not wash. Blood will be answered.

Abraham Lincoln, in his Second Inaugural Address, spoke of the Civil War as a punishment visited on this country for the evil of human slavery. Every drop of blood drawn by the surgeon's sword in this day will be repaid. We are living in the midst of a transgression against laws drafted before the world was made and written on tablets of more than stone.

The principles forged in hearts on Sinai sealed a covenant between God and Moses. "I call heaven and earth to witness against you today. I have set before you life or death, blessing or a curse. Oh, that you would choose life that you and your children and your children's children might live."

We are a people whose forebears, with hope and faith, some in chains, in small, frail, crowded boats, crossed the oceans when they were wider than the stars are far apart. Each of us is the product of a distressful pregnancy at some point in our chain of existence. We were the unwanted of Europe, Asia, and Africa. Our history and our heritage cries out and says, "We cannot go without God." If we betray our heritage of bravery, hardship, and honor by telling the child that there is no room in the inn, we will find that we are a people without a destiny. There will be no room for us in the stars.

Let us send a message from the shores of the Atlantic Ocean to the vast expanse of the Pacific, from the Gulf of Mexico to the Canadian border, that even as King George, the crown, and parliament were out of step with the interests and concerns of the early colonists, so too are many leaders out of step with the moral concerns of grass-roots Americans. On the issue of the slaughter of the innocents, we direct attention to the recent Connecticut Mutual Insurance survey which reveals that only 29 percent of elected and appointed officials believe abortion is morally wrong, but that 65 percent of all Americans and 74 percent of religious Americans believe that abortion is morally wrong. We have hope and assurance that because our cause is right, it will prevail. Hence, we thrive rather than wither in the face of adversity. Our commitment springs to life from the blood and suffering of the dying millions of little helpless ones. We represent an absolute commitment to an absolute cause. We are a rebuke to the intellectual barbarians who preach and uphold the ethic of killing for the most trivial of reasons.

An unspeakable miscarriage of justice has been engineered by the intellectual barbarians. Though the wheels of God grind slowly, they grind exceedingly fine. The American people will thwart the murderous acts of the intellectual barbarians by exercising their wonderful citizenship privileges of praying, obtaining information, working, voting, and claiming God's promise found in 2nd Chronicles 7:14—"If my people, which are called by my name, shall humble themselves, and pray and seek my face and turn from their wicked ways; then will I hear from heaven and forgive their sin, and will heal their land."

The program of the Christian political movement also calls for the implementation of a biblical view of economics. We stand unalterably opposed to deficit spending by government at any level, for any purpose short of a dire national emergency.

Recent history has demonstrated that deficit spending for ostensibly noble purposes runs its course and results in the plunder of the masses through monetary inflation. The Word of

105

God warns of the severe judgment of Almighty God against the nation that pursues its own self-interests while grinding the faces of the poor (Isaiah 1:23; 3:14-15).

While the Bible repeatedly warns of divine judgment against the nation that robs and plunders the poor, and deprives them of justice, nowhere does it authorize governments to forcibly expropriate the earnings of the more resourceful and wealthy classes and to transfer such earnings to the poorer classes in the pattern of the modern "welfare state."

The Bible advocates generous private sector, church, and family aid to the unfortunate, but nowhere provides any basis for taxing the "haves" and giving to the "have-nots," as Lyndon Johnson once put it.

The mass plunder of American citizens in the name of the welfare state in recent decades has tended to demotivate the "haves" by robbing them and to demotivate and destroy the "have-nots" by locking them into a hopeless condition of dependency. Now, the inflation which has resulted in considerable part from "welfare state" policies wreaks its ravages on all of our citizens.

Americans who participate in the Christian political movement believe that the divine law of the harvest is of necessity being invoked. Those who have sown the seeds of plunder are themselves being extricated from public office these days as the people awake to an awareness of the tragic consequences of their evil deeds.

Various objections to the Christian political movement are being raised by certain elements of the media these days.

First, we are being labeled an "extremist movement of the right." This is a strange charge, inasmuch as we adhere unalterably to the U.S. Constitution and to a strict constructionist approach in the interpretation of it. Has America moved so far to the left that those who now call her back to her own constitutional foundations must be regarded as right-wing extremists? If such be the case, God help us!

Second, the objection is made that the Christian political movement is Ayatollah-like, Nazi-like, coercive and ruthless, and that its ascendancy would deprive the nation of its freedoms.

The fact of the matter is that those who unburden themselves of such unflattering charges have departed from truth and reality. If indeed there is any obstacle to the implementation of Nazi-like and Ayatollah-like policies in America, it is the Christian political movement. There was no such movement in Germany at the time of the rise of Hitler, none in Russia or China when the Communists took over, and none in Iran to stand in the way of Khomeini.

In the long sweep of history it has been demonstrated

abundantly that those who are doctrinally and constitutionally opposed to tyranny, as are biblically-committed Christians, will raise the greatest standard against it. The freedom movement in the Soviet Union is a prime contemporary example of this principle.

Looking back over the decades of this century, it is evident that biblical concepts of human rights, responsible freedom, and enlightened justice have not held sway, but rather have been repudiated, in the statist tyrannies imposed by the Fascist, Nazi, Communist, and Moslem regimes which have terrorized, brutalized, victimized, and enslaved their populations.

In the third place, it is alleged that the Christian political movement is advocating an unconstitutional position which violates the time-honored doctrine of the separation of church and state. Here again, our critics have departed from the truth.

An act of Congress establishing an official state church, or denying any church the right to exist, would constitute a direct violation of church-state separation as defined in the First Amendment. Likewise, under court interpretations of the First Amendment, the endorsement of candidates or dictation of government policy by an organized church body would violate church-state separation.

On the other hand, the consistent exercise of citizenship responsibility by Christian Americans individually and in co-operative association with one another outside the institutional church is wholly consistent with First Amendment doctrine. Christians are also citizens. When we register to vote, support the candidate of our choice, and otherwise exercise the prerogatives of citizenship, we simply claim the rights which belong to all Americans. We perceive such activities as a biblically-ordained service for God, and we will not be intimidated from rendering such service. Those strident voices of pseudo-liberalism which seek to neutralize us by deceptive tactics will not succeed.

Reference was made earlier to the findings of the Connecticut Mutual Life Insurance Company's survey to determine American values in the 1980s. Based on those findings, the outlook for the Christian political movement is bright. The unique study, undertaken by Research and Forecasts, Inc., of New York for Connecticut Mutual, concluded that religion "has penetrated virtually every dimension of American experience" and is "a stronger determinant of our values" than any other factor. In fact, the report stated that moral issues have, "via religion, vaulted to the forefront of the political dialogue" and "something unusual is happening." Said Dr. John C. Pollock, the project's research director, "It's more than a movement. It's something running through the whole culture."

The massive 337-page report concluded: "Our findings

107

suggest that the increasing impact of religion on our social and political institutions may be only the beginning of a trend that could change the face of America."

Already a significant factor in American life, there is every reason to believe the Christian political movement will continue to experience dynamic growth and to exert a pervasive influence.

Regardless of what may be the opinion of those who view the movement from the outside, those who are positioned within its ranks are convinced it is helping to call the nation back to her spiritual heritage, and to lay the foundation for a better America in the decades ahead.

Church-State Relations:
A Black Feminist's Perspective
by Ruth H. Charity

    Long active in the civil rights movement and a past Democratic National Committeewoman from Virginia, Ruth H. Charity addresses the church-state issue based on her political experience and her close association with black American churches. Charity agrees with McAteer that it is appropriate for Christians to be involved in the political sector. She believes that the oppression of black Americans has been ameliorated historically by the strong cultural and political role which the black church has played. Her emphasis is on the need to continue the struggle for equality in America as a top priority with which Christians should concern themselves.

Church-state relations is one of the crucial issues of our time. Changes are occurring or have occurred in the religious-political community which make the old order which said that "politics has no business in the church" obsolete. Today, politics is the business of the church. We are now surrounded by a concept called "moral majority" which is essentially political.

As an individual who has lived under a Baptist minister father all of her life, I believe that I can view contemporary church-state relations in depth, especially from a black perspective. As a black woman political activist, I would approach this subject by asking three questions: first, regarding the position of the black church, "Where does it fit into the picture, and should we accept the fact that politics is and must be a part of its ministry?" Second, "Have the women of this generation impacted on the church and made known to the church as well as the governmental system the issues which vitally concern women today?" Third, "What kind of impact does Moral Majority have on the church and politics?"

I

The issue of separation of church and state has been pervasive in our society, particularly from the black perspective, for there have always been some good church members who would say, "Politics and government have no place in this church," while at the same time these same people were out fighting the ills of society. It is well known that the foundation and backbone of the Civil Rights Movement was the black church. In fact, many of our early seekers of political and public office were black ministers. So the issue, "Where does the black church stand on the question of church-state relations and politics?" seems quite clear to me, since the black church, for years, has been the center of all positive activity in the black community. It must, today more than ever before, continue to be a beacon light for understanding the social and moral issues of the day, a center for educating its members on how politics affect their daily lives, and a center of faith and hope that through positive action our system and all of its people will be better off politically and spiritually.

Historically, the black church has been the foundation of the

from the realism of the day, or from the issues of the
[...]h people must demonstrate the love of God and the
[...]d of man in the marketplace as well as the church. The
[...]st be in the forefront of educating the people on the
[...]confront them in a broad, fair-minded way, for if our
[...]o be real, then our religious institutions must deal with
[...]ues of the world. We must teach our members how to
[...]ese issues, respecting the rights of all. Maybe one of
[...]s people think politics and government are dirty,
[...]d negative in general, is because the "good church
[...]t involve themselves more in either knowledge or
[...]n.

[...]urch has the unique opportunity to impact on political
[...]n clear unbiased attitudes that other special interests
[...] it is unfortunate when it does not face up to this
[...]ty. However, the bulk of opinion seems to indicate
[...]rch is expanding its outreach to all people. The doors
[...] cracked to permit a poor person, a black person, a
[...] comes from other points of the world speaking a
[...]nguage or possessing a different heritage, and even a
[...]rican, to enter to worship, to be comforted, and to be
[...]ssage and the mission Jesus Christ came to bring.
[...]hurch, including all denominations, sees and feels the
[...]h local, state, and national as well as international
[...]forces have on its people, and the people outside its
[...]st assume its responsibility not only to render unto
[...]ings that are God's, but to render unto Caesar those
[...]re Caesar's. In doing so it must make sure that the
[...]sar are not totalitarian in effect, or destructive of the
[...] and spirit of man, God's greatest creation. The
[...]f Christ and the philosophy of politics will and must
[...]r to benefit, to save, mankind from ultimate destruc-
[...]ternal violence and internal explosion. Once again,
[...] of man will become the focus of reality rather than
[...]he focus of reality.
[...]ch has a new opportunity to give new leadership to
[...]ether it be black or white, the church must speak on
[...]t affect all of the people of this country, including
[...] the capacity to impact on our political leaders in a
[...]it summons its will to follow true concerns for the
[...]n, as Jesus Christ came to do.
[...]e only hope that mankind has today, because there
[...]separate compartments to life. Life has to be lived
[...]s a single entity. The church must also be a single
[...]s resources to promote the value of life in the realm
[...]ion.

black community. Out of it came education. The church Sunday School extended itself into reading, writing, and arithmetic. It branched out to form separate institutions from kindergarten to college. Out of it came civic responsibility, for it urged its citizens to register and vote. In the days of the poll tax, it had voter registration clubs to assist its members in saving up that $1.50 and taught them how to fill out the registration forms. Out of the black church came economic growth because its ministers encouraged its members to work diligently, save their money, buy homes, educate their children, and become self-sufficient.

The black community had no civic clubs and associations to take care of its needs in a world in which it was ill-prepared to function. It had no firsthand knowledge of organization and how to influence the financial and political institutions of our country. Thus, from the days of earliest slavery, since this was the only institution blacks were allowed to have, the church nurtured and cared for black people's needs in every way. It not only told black people how to get the pie in the sky, but how to get some pie here on earth. The black church, more than perhaps any other institution, teaches the equality of human beings; a truth, a philosophy, that has helped black people to survive. The black church involvement in the Civil Rights Movement was a very simple means of getting Americans to live up to the words in the Bill of Rights and the Constitution while trying to promote the brotherhood of man and the fatherhood of God.

II

Women have the responsibility of helping the church to understand the necessity for the Equal Rights Amendment, especially in view of all the outlandish interpretations of the law which have come from persons who either do not understand the proposed law or who are insensitive to myriad discriminations against women. Many women who are the victims of discrimination have been so brainwashed that they do not know or understand the inequalities to which they and other women are subjected. Nowhere is it written in the Holy Bible that women are to be the doormats of man. Woman was created to be the helpmate of man. When we look at great women in the Bible, we find Lydia, who was a businesswoman. Providing the first church outside of the Judean area, she opened her house so that the teachings of Jesus could be brought to the gentiles.

The church should be the strongest ally of the Equal Rights Amendment. It is morally wrong for anyone to ever try to suggest that women are inferior beings.

The exploiters of women still want them to be second-class citizens. In spite of the equal pay for equal work law, they want to be free to pay women less than men who are doing the same or less work. They want to keep women away from the top positions in industry, business, and local, state, and national government. It is time now to make known to national legislators and state legislators that women must be treated equally and legally protected through amendment of the Constitution by the Equal Rights Amendment, which simply states, "Equality of rights under the law shall not be denied or abridged by the United States or by any state on account of sex."

III

Finally, we are now faced more strongly than ever with political activity in the church because of the activities of Moral Majority. Moral Majority, through its chief spokesperson and founder, the Rev. Jerry Falwell, is using politics in the church not as an educational tool but as a power tool to dominate the operation of the national government. It is one thing to support the government, point out its deficiencies, and help those responsible for its operation in a cooperative, constructive way, but another matter when the entire government is to be undertaken and an effort made to dominate, reshape, reform, and re-create the government according to a master plan.

An article written by Johnny Greene, in *Playboy* magazine of January 1981, quotes one of the proponents of Moral Majority, the Rev. Robert Billings, as saying, "People want leadership. They don't know what to think themselves. They want to be told what to think by those of us here close to the front." Another of the leaders of the new moral right, Gary Potter, in the same article, is quoted as saying, "When the Christian Majority takes over this country, there will be no satanic churches, no more free distribution of pornography, no more abortion on demand, and no more talk of rights for homosexuals. After the Christian majority takes control, pluralism will be seen as immoral and evil and the state will not permit anybody the right to practice evil." Even Jesus Christ did not undertake to regulate society with an iron hand. God created man with a free will to choose between good and evil, to be evil or to accept salvation.

Moral Majority is headed for what some allege will be a Christian dictatorship. A dictatorship is reprehensible, whether by Hitler, Mussolini, Stalin, or the church.

Mr. Billings and Mr. Potter, as they work with other members of the New Right, seek to impose their ideas and will upon us through legislation which they call the Family Protection Act. They, through it, are about the business of designing a new moral society for the United States and want to define what would and would not be tolerated by the far-right dictatorship they envision.

This danger is even more frightening when we see the

President of the United States
has to call Jerry Falwell abou
Supreme Court of the United
Dr. Ronald S. Godwin, vice pr
of Moral Majority, said, "Rea
Judge O'Connor met the stan
own personal stand on aborti
is Falwell to be assured? Wha
opposed to any other religiou

The black church has sp
Moral Majority through t
President of the National Pa
Rev. Jerry Falwell with "pe
Gravely, Executive Director
Virginia, is right when he
Majority and the Moral Maj

In my humble opinion
concepts of the politicall
Majority. Many wonder ho
o'clock on Sunday morning
America, and yet, Moral
morality of people concerni
all of the other politically s
examination, we find that
dictatorship but also racial

The Rev. Jerry Falwel
Gospel Hour" that abortion
schools were violations o
defined that moral law. H
communities fight pornogr
textbooks and other burnin
extracts millions of dollar
politicians who are or are
plan to reshape American

I do not agree with the
what they believe in. Whe
money and power to est
people and religion as a
danger this country has b
American people had be
tionalism and the religiou
media preachers whom
they raise so much money

Our religious leader
right, nay, a duty, to inv
issues before us, right her
the contemporary churc

sanctuary
day. Chur
brotherhoo
church mu
issues that
religion is t
the real iss
deal with t
the reason
crooked, a
folk" do no
participatic

The ch
leaders wit
do not, and
responsibil
that the chu
are slightly
person who
different la
native Ame
given the me

As the c
impact whic
policies and
doors, it mu
God those th
things that
things of Cae
mind, body,
philosophy c
come togethe
tion from ex
the humanity
things being

The chu
mankind. Wh
the issues th
women. It ha
broad way if
welfare of ma

This is th
are no longer
and viewed a
entity using it
of political ac

black community. Out of it came education. The church Sunday School extended itself into reading, writing, and arithmetic. It branched out to form separate institutions from kindergarten to college. Out of it came civic responsibility, for it urged its citizens to register and vote. In the days of the poll tax, it had voter registration clubs to assist its members in saving up that $1.50 and taught them how to fill out the registration forms. Out of the black church came economic growth because its ministers encouraged its members to work diligently, save their money, buy homes, educate their children, and become self-sufficient.

The black community had no civic clubs and associations to take care of its needs in a world in which it was ill-prepared to function. It had no firsthand knowledge of organization and how to influence the financial and political institutions of our country. Thus, from the days of earliest slavery, since this was the only institution blacks were allowed to have, the church nurtured and cared for black people's needs in every way. It not only told black people how to get the pie in the sky, but how to get some pie here on earth. The black church, more than perhaps any other institution, teaches the equality of human beings; a truth, a philosophy, that has helped black people to survive. The black church involvement in the Civil Rights Movement was a very simple means of getting Americans to live up to the words in the Bill of Rights and the Constitution while trying to promote the brotherhood of man and the fatherhood of God.

II

Women have the responsibility of helping the church to understand the necessity for the Equal Rights Amendment, especially in view of all the outlandish interpretations of the law which have come from persons who either do not understand the proposed law or who are insensitive to myriad discriminations against women. Many women who are the victims of discrimination have been so brainwashed that they do not know or understand the inequalities to which they and other women are subjected. Nowhere is it written in the Holy Bible that women are to be the doormats of man. Woman was created to be the helpmate of man. When we look at great women in the Bible, we find Lydia, who was a businesswoman. Providing the first church outside of the Judean area, she opened her house so that the teachings of Jesus could be brought to the gentiles.

The church should be the strongest ally of the Equal Rights Amendment. It is morally wrong for anyone to ever try to suggest that women are inferior beings.

The exploiters of women still want them to be second-class citizens. In spite of the equal pay for equal work law, they want to be free to pay women less than men who are doing the same or

111

less work. They want to keep women away from the top positions in industry, business, and local, state, and national government. It is time now to make known to national legislators and state legislators that women must be treated equally and legally protected through amendment of the Constitution by the Equal Rights Amendment, which simply states, "Equality of rights under the law shall not be denied or abridged by the United States or by any state on account of sex."

III

Finally, we are now faced more strongly than ever with political activity in the church because of the activities of Moral Majority. Moral Majority, through its chief spokesperson and founder, the Rev. Jerry Falwell, is using politics in the church not as an educational tool but as a power tool to dominate the operation of the national government. It is one thing to support the government, point out its deficiencies, and help those responsible for its operation in a cooperative, constructive way, but another matter when the entire government is to be undertaken and an effort made to dominate, reshape, reform, and re-create the government according to a master plan.

An article written by Johnny Greene, in *Playboy* magazine of January 1981, quotes one of the proponents of Moral Majority, the Rev. Robert Billings, as saying, "People want leadership. They don't know what to think themselves. They want to be told what to think by those of us here close to the front." Another of the leaders of the new moral right, Gary Potter, in the same article, is quoted as saying, "When the Christian Majority takes over this country, there will be no satanic churches, no more free distribution of pornography, no more abortion on demand, and no more talk of rights for homosexuals. After the Christian majority takes control, pluralism will be seen as immoral and evil and the state will not permit anybody the right to practice evil." Even Jesus Christ did not undertake to regulate society with an iron hand. God created man with a free will to choose between good and evil, to be evil or to accept salvation.

Moral Majority is headed for what some allege will be a Christian dictatorship. A dictatorship is reprehensible, whether by Hitler, Mussolini, Stalin, or the church.

Mr. Billings and Mr. Potter, as they work with other members of the New Right, seek to impose their ideas and will upon us through legislation which they call the Family Protection Act. They, through it, are about the business of designing a new moral society for the United States and want to define what would and would not be tolerated by the far-right dictatorship they envision.

This danger is even more frightening when we see the

President of the United States so influenced by this group that he has to call Jerry Falwell about his selection of a nominee for the Supreme Court of the United States. Spokesperson for the group, Dr. Ronald S. Godwin, vice president and chief operations officer of Moral Majority, said, "Reagan wanted to assure Falwell that Judge O'Connor met the standards and is in agreement with his own personal stand on abortion, ERA, and what have you." Who is Falwell to be assured? What is Moral Majority to be assured as opposed to any other religious or secular organization?

The black church has spoken out against the philosophy of Moral Majority through the Rev. William Augustus Jones, President of the National Pastor's Conference, who charges the Rev. Jerry Falwell with "perverting the Christian faith." Jack Gravely, Executive Director of the NAACP State Conference in Virginia, is right when he says, "Falwell, President of Moral Majority and the Moral Majority are very dangerous."

In my humble opinion, there is a difference between the concepts of the politically active black church and Moral Majority. Many wonder how morally right is it when eleven o'clock on Sunday morning is still the most segregated hour in America, and yet, Moral Majority is trying to re-design the morality of people concerning ERA, abortion, school busing, and all of the other politically sensitive issues of the day. Upon close examination, we find that Moral Majority smacks not only of dictatorship but also racial and religious prejudice.

The Rev. Jerry Falwell stated to viewers of the "Old-Time Gospel Hour" that abortion and "secular humanism" in the public schools were violations of a "moral law" although he never defined that moral law. He claimed that he was "helping local communities fight pornography, homosexuality, obscene school textbooks and other burning issues." Meanwhile, Moral Majority extracts millions of dollars from the public to support or defeat politicians who are or are not in accord with their new dictatorial plan to reshape American society.

I do not agree with their position, but they have a right to say what they believe in. When it comes to a calculated design with money and power to establish a dictatorship using Christian people and religion as a front, however, we have the greatest danger this country has been confronted with in its history. The American people had better not be carried away by the emotionalism and the religious fervor of Falwell and other electronic media preachers whom Gravely called "pulpit pimps" because they raise so much money on television.

Our religious leaders and our religious institutions have a right, nay, a duty, to involve people in thinking about the great issues before us, right here on earth. There is a place for politics in the contemporary church because the church should not be a sanctuary from the realism of the day, or from the issues of the day. Church people must demonstrate the love of God and the brotherhood of man in the marketplace as well as the church. The church must be in the forefront of educating the people on the issues that confront them in a broad, fair-minded way, for if our religion is to be real, then our religious institutions must deal with the real issues of the world. We must teach our members how to deal with these issues, respecting the rights of all. Maybe one of the reasons people think politics and government are dirty, crooked, and negative in general, is because the "good church folk" do not involve themselves more in either knowledge or participation.

The church has the unique opportunity to impact on political leaders with clear unbiased attitudes that other special interests do not, and it is unfortunate when it does not face up to this responsibility. However, the bulk of opinion seems to indicate that the church is expanding its outreach to all people. The doors are slightly cracked to permit a poor person, a black person, a person who comes from other points of the world speaking a different language or possessing a different heritage, and even a native American, to enter to worship, to be comforted, and to be given the message and the mission Jesus Christ came to bring.

As the church, including all denominations, sees and feels the impact which local, state, and national as well as international policies and forces have on its people, and the people outside its doors, it must assume its responsibility not only to render unto God those things that are God's, but to render unto Caesar those things that are Caesar's. In doing so it must make sure that the things of Caesar are not totalitarian in effect, or destructive of the mind, body, and spirit of man, God's greatest creation. The philosophy of Christ and the philosophy of politics will and must come together to benefit, to *save*, mankind from ultimate destruction from external violence and internal explosion. Once again, the humanity of man will become the focus of reality rather than things being the focus of reality.

The church has a new opportunity to give new leadership to mankind. Whether it be black or white, the church must speak on the issues that affect all of the people of this country, including women. It has the capacity to impact on our political leaders in a broad way if it summons its will to follow true concerns for the welfare of man, as Jesus Christ came to do.

This is the only hope that mankind has today, because there are no longer separate compartments to life. Life has to be lived and viewed as a single entity. The church must also be a single entity using its resources to promote the value of life in the realm of political action.

The Prospects for an
Emerging Christian Consensus
by G. William Whitehurst

*Congressman G. William Whitehurst agrees with McAteer
that the Christian political movement has had success in selection
of candidates and in influencing local political party structures.
He believes strongly, however, that the test of the success of the
right-wing Christians will be how successful they are in attract-
ing a majority of the electorate to their issues. To the extent that
they can capitalize on issues which will appeal to non-church
goers, they have a bright future. "There are millions of Americans
who haven't seen the inside of a church for years who are equally
unhappy for many of the same reasons" as Moral Majority, he
contends. Congress, however, is likely to act slowly on legislation
which has enormous significance for Americans' future. The new
Christian right must be seen as important, but it is only "one
factor in the equation of ongoing change."*

The appearance of a strongly conservative Christian political movement as a factor in American political life may appear to have been a sudden and puzzling phenomenon. In reality, its birth is in no way surprising, given the changing standards and mores during this generation.

I saw the stirrings of it about five years ago and have watched with interest its rapid growth since. As an officeholder, I am keenly sensitive to any new political force in my district or in the nation, and I have seen at first hand the impact of this new Christian bloc on my party.

I am a believer in God and my outlook on moral issues is strongly influenced by my basic Christian faith. So when I am confronted in Congress with a matter having moral overtones, my view is going to be somewhat subjective. I assume similar reactions among all of my colleagues, whatever their religious or ethical convictions.

I do not believe that it is possible nor desirable to expect that lawmakers, or indeed anyone in a position of trust, should endeavor to behave in a spiritually schizophrenic way. In fact, members of the House of Representatives would be hypocrites if they did not act in accordance with their own convictions.

The words of our national motto are affixed in brass on the marble backdrop behind the Speaker's chair. No member or visitor in the chamber can avoid being reminded that "In God We Trust."

The conservative Christian political movement came about as a reaction to new, and what were perceived to be threatening, influences in American life. The birth of organizations like Moral Majority, for example, has not been spontaneous, or, forgive the phrase, an evolutionary result of fundamental Christian activism. It has happened because of the concern of a majority of our 40 million Bible-oriented citizens that the nation's traditional goals and values are in jeopardy. This is made clear by the statistics cited by Edward McAteer from the Connecticut Life Insurance survey. These 40 million Americans perceive that a succession of elected officials, from the president on down, have either initiated or tolerated decisions or laws inconsistent with the Judeo-Christian standards predominant in American society for most of our history.

As both a participant and an observer in the political arena, I have been interested in the ability of conservative Christian activists to make their influence felt so quickly. Like other groups that have desired to promote their own objectives, they have done so more effectively in the nominating and selection process than at the ballot box.

To be sure, there have been elections recently, some at the Congressional level, in which conservative Christian activists have determined the outcome by their numbers. But in most cases, their percentage of the total number of voters has not been sufficient to make the difference. Where they have been highly successful has been in the choosing of candidates, and here their adroitness has surprised the so-called "pros," the party regulars who have traditionally dominated the party structure and named the candidates.

It would be easy for me to digress at this point and cite a number of recent examples of the power exercised at Republican mass meetings, district conventions, and finally the state convention itself. The conservative-Christian coalition rolled forward like a juggernaut, its leaders as confident in maneuvering blocs of delegates as any political mainstay whose party affiliation stretches back to Alf Landon.

Of course, there have been other new forces, groups, coalitions, and the like that have burst upon the scene and dominated party conventions throughout our history. They have carried a variety of banners and have championed a host of causes. It says something for party resiliency in America that the parties, Democratic and Republican, have absorbed them or survived them, as the case might be. One has to go back to the political role exercised by the Methodist Bishop James Cannon in Virginia politics in the 1920s to find a parallel for what we are experiencing in party affairs now, but Cannon's influence was restricted largely to prohibition.

This participation in, and in some cases, domination of, a party by conservative Christian activists is new. It has not been without friction and in some cases resentment by the regulars. That is perfectly natural, since a certain amount of jealousy and power play is a part of any political organization. The main question is, how long will this conservative Christian activism sustain itself? Can it, or does it desire to, take over the party structure where it may be in a position to do so?

This Christian political movement has engendered fears. The Rev. Falwell's Moral Majority has certainly borne the brunt of the counterattacks that have been launched, and it would seem that he has welcomed them. But this reaction was to be expected. Believers and non-believers, liberals and conservatives alike, have expressed alarm over the role of religious activists in

117

political affairs. In spite of the emotions generated on both sides, I think that we can only say that honest people can disagree.

Two final aspects need to be emphasized. Obviously, the Republican Party has been more directly affected by the conservative Christian movement than its Democratic counterpart. Parenthetically, I would observe that the Democratic Party was strongly influenced in the 1960s by the Rev. Martin Luther King's black activism. There is a parallel that can be drawn between the two.

It is a matter of keeping them in perspective. Moreover, the new political Christians are not alone in their discontent over the drift away from traditional values. There are millions of Americans who haven't seen the inside of a church for years who are equally unhappy for many of the same reasons, be they economic or social. Christian activists are simply more visible because they are vocal and outspoken—and they are organized. For these reasons, their opponents and critics regard them as a danger. In reality, they are simply the cutting edge of the pendulum, which, having reached its left-most limit, is now swinging rapidly back to the right. It is hard to imagine that this group could have succeeded in the period of the sixties or early seventies. Those were different times.

The conservative Christian political movement must be viewed only in the context of other forces. These are dynamic times, and this political activism is but one factor in the equation of ongoing change.

Finally, what can be expected in the way of legislative action as a result of conservative Christian activism? Here the movement is confronted with a different challenge from that of bringing adherents to mass meetings or sending delegates to state or national conventions. The 40 million Americans who believe that the nation's values are in jeopardy are indeed a mighty army, but they do not all march to the same drumbeat, as some might expect.

Furthermore, those 40 million are part of a 230-million entity, which dilutes their strength. Clearly, they have potential political strength. The conservative Christian political movement and the black Christian church activists can muster considerable force in pressing their views on elected officials. Letters and postcards can be generated by the thousands on behalf of an issue, but these come in torrents from other organizations and groups, with other views, as well.

In spite of the opinion, widely held, that congressmen are an unenlightened breed, nothing could be further from the truth. Running every two years compels an incumbent intent on remaining one to fine tune his senses and instincts. There are nuances to the issues of abortion, prayer in school, and tuition tax credits that complicate their legislative resolution. It is relatively easy to be categorical about broad issues but far less so to draft laws, especially those that will both reflect a consensus and stand the constitutional test.

Thus the Congress, at least in its current makeup, is likely to proceed slowly in these areas. And I would suspect that the president, in spite of his so far unqualified success with his economic legislative program, will proceed cautiously. For in the final analysis, it is a consensus that must be found, whether we are dealing with a change in our tax laws or one of the issues perceived as critical by any politically involved group, no matter what its origins.

It was a consensus of concern, after all, that spawned the conservative Christian political movement. Now that it is a viable force it will have an opportunity to press for its goals. The pattern of its success will depend upon its effectiveness in convincing a majority of the electorate that their interests coincide with its own. That is the strength and the genius of the American political system.

Politics and Religion
by Sen. Jeremiah A. Denton, Jr.

Jeremiah A. Denton, Jr., was elected to the United States Senate in 1980. Since taking office, he has come to be perceived by some as the leading "watchdog" over the nation's morals. As an Alabama Republican and Roman Catholic, Denton's conservative credentials are impeccable.

In his essay, "Politics and Religion," Denton defends the right of people with religious convictions to engage in political affairs as a means of achieving their moral goals. He maintains that the "wall of separation" between church and state should properly be defined as a "line of separation" between the two. Basing much of his personal view upon the adage that "character is fate," Denton expresses concern over what he thinks is a decline in public morality, and concludes by insisting that morality in public affairs cannot be expected to survive exclusive of religious principles.

Relying on what I hope is common sense and some study and observations, I would begin by offering a general opinion of relevance: no matter where each of us stands in his or her definition of the proper relationship between church and state, between religion and politics, I believe at least 98 percent of us would agree that a person's moral principles affect the way he thinks and the way he acts. Principles are important. Principles may not always govern our thoughts and actions, but they affect them. Someone has even gone so far as to say "character is fate." In other words, all other things being equal, a person's life, happiness, and success or failure (at least in the person's eyes) will be determined or predetermined by his selection of principles.

Again, all other things being equal, the same generalization may be applied to a nation. Its principles will predetermine its success. Hence, my intense interest in national principles. In that sense, the United States' traditional principles look pretty good. Indeed, a case can be made that all nations generally principled by the Judeo-Christian ethic have done relatively well.

I

As H. Richard Niebuhr has pointed out in his insightful book, *The Social Sources of Denominationalism*, religious institutions are in flux. Within the last few years, the restructuring of denominations and the dialectic within every major denomination have been dramatic.

Some religious groups seem to be retrenching constantly, while new groups are growing apace, and still others have become revitalized. As some congregations have become too scholarly and arcane, new ones with the institutional energy and relative youth of teenagers have arisen to take their places. As the Methodist Church emerged from the Church of England, so the Church of the Nazarene has emerged from the Methodist Church.

The last few years have seen a new and widespread interest in religion and morality, but the revitalization has not extended across the board. The decline in attendance and support of many upper-middle-class mainline Protestant churches continues. But there has been a marked growth among the groups that seem to offer more surety and simplicity—for example, among the Churches of God, evangelical Protestants, traditional Catholics, and independent television preachers.

The political expressions of these growing groups have been greeted with delight from some and dismay from others. Most recently in the news has been the blanket condemnation of Moral Majority by the president of Yale, Bart Giamatti, who said that group had made a "political assault on religious and political freedoms in the United States."

The last twenty years have also seen a restructuring of political groups in the United States. In 1951, there were very few Catholics or Jews in the Republican Party. There were very few Southerners, as well, so the Republican Party had a very narrow base. The movement of Catholics, Jews, and Southern Protestants away from their traditional alignment with the Democratic Party began in the late 1950s and culminated in the 1980 election. In that election, there were no fewer than five Catholics elected to the Senate as Republicans—something which would have been unthinkable twenty years ago.

I cite that only as an example of my point that, in the last few years, there has been a restructuring of the political order in this country in regard to various religious groups. Social and moral conservatives have tended to gravitate toward the Republican Party, for whatever reason. That change was reflected in the election, and I believe that trend will continue.

The questions have been asked: does this mean the Republican Party will become a narrow sectarian party like some of those in Israel? What should be the interaction of politics and religion? Whatever happened to the alleged "wall of separation" between church and state?

II

In September 1981, President Sadat of Egypt instituted a massive crackdown on religious extremists and political opponents. In a three-hour televised speech to the Egyptian Parliament, he hammered home the main theme again and again: "No politics in religion and no religion in politics."

Our neighbor to the south—Mexico—had a similar experience in the 1850s. Prior to that time, the Catholic Church had such enormous wealth and power that it overshadowed the government of Mexico. Finally, the church and state were separated so completely that it is still a violation of Mexican law for a clergyman to wear his vestments or even a clerical collar in public. When Pope John Paul II visited Mexico, the government blinked its eyes to avoid having to fine or imprison the pontiff. But that was a very rare bending of the law.

In the seventeenth century, Roger Williams began what he called a "livilie experiment" in Rhode Island and established his so-called "wall of separation" between church and state.

In 1802, President Jefferson, in a letter to the Banbury, Connecticut, Baptist Convention, picked up Williams' language about a wall of separation between church and state. To the lay public, that phrase has unfortunately become part of the American political collective unconscious, if I may modify a Jungian term. And, indeed, the phrase may well express the position of Jefferson and Madison, who were very suspicious of the power of the clergy and who took a very hard line. Madison even believed that it was a mistake to have chaplains for the armed service. But eight years after the death of Jefferson, Madison wrote that he had to admit "...that it may not be easy, in every possible case, to trace the line of separation between the rights of religion and the Civil Authority with such distinctness as to avoid collisions and doubts on unessential points."

The phrase "wall of separation" has had great currency, but it has also produced much confusion and conflict. That phrase helped perpetuate thinking about the situation with concepts that are not really applicable to the American constitutional scheme. To me, a "wall" conjures up something very tangible and solid, built to last without change.

Madison's words, "the line of separation between the rights of religion and the Civil Authority" are much more precisely descriptive. Madison's word "line" unlike Williams' "wall" does not conjure up the image of a solid and unchanging structure built by the Founders, but rather a "path of a moving point, thought of as having length but not breadth," as my dictionary explains it. Furthermore, the concept of a "line" unlike that of a "wall" permits one to think of a point constantly moving and even zigzagging, and therefore, as Madison noted, not always easy to trace "with such distinctness as to avoid collisions and doubts."

If we think of the American situation with Williams' concepts of "church," "state," and a "wall," the image in my mind is that of two distinct and settled institutions in a society once and for all time separated by a clearly defined and impenetrable barrier with solid foundations in the Constitution. If we use this model, we are not far from Sadat's vision of church and state. In the beginning, no one knew, nor could know, just where the line between them was or would be because no one could anticipate the proliferation of differing institutional forms of religion or the various faces of civil authority. In the eighteenth century, there were few precedents for a free society to serve as guidelines.

If we use the model of a "line," we must find where the line or lines may be drawn between the religious and the political. The Constitution and the First Amendment laid down very general principles to define the relationship between religion and politics. What these principles would mean in practice no one could anticipate. That was left to be determined by our national courts.

123

In my judgment, the newly formed link between the religious right and the political right does not pose a constitutional threat. This link simply expresses the constitutional guarantee of free exercise of religion.

My understanding of constitutional history indicates that religion was intended to be a neutral factor within the formal bounds of government; however, it did provide inspiration to the writers of the Constitution, and was the source of their rationale. I think the debate as recorded from that time would substantiate this point. The writers of the Constitution simply chose to place religion beyond the authority of the federal government. You cannot legislate morality, but you can legislate from morality.

The object of the Constitution writers was to protect the young government from formally imposing on government a national religion, not to protect the government from men or morality, nor to subtract away traditional moral principles [sic]. The American memory of pervasive and powerful state churches in Europe and New England was too fresh to ignore the threat of organized religion. Religion need not be tightly organized to be a powerful force. Religion was, in the eighteenth century, and is today, a power center, a force to be reckoned with in the political as well as the spiritual arena. The spontaneous response of a million Americans to an effective television ministry is a powerful force today. This is not to say that there are not other power centers. Television journalism, organized labor, and big business are three very powerful influences in our country today.

III

Morality is the foundation of any enduring society. This nation has a long and distinguished history of men and women of morality who have molded the social and political scene as a direct result of their faith. This country cannot afford to segregate religious leaders from politics. I remind you that there is no political issue without a moral dimension; that there is no moral issue without a political consequence. Our religious beliefs not only affect the way we think, but the way we live, legislate, and judge, as well as lead in government.

However, conspicuous sociological consequences of immorality in the past fifteen years or so have forced many religious persons to speak up, to speak out against immorality and amorality in government. I believe most of the objections which have been raised to the new activism of these people are simply a reflection of differing political ideologies. In other words, liberals are objecting to the actions of conservative Christians just as conservatives have objected to such organizations as the World Council of Churches. It depends on whose ox is being gored.

Some people have misinterpreted the constitutional provision for the separation of church and state; they have interpreted it to mean that religious people should not get involved in government affairs. Of course, that is contrary to the tradition of this country. To bar persons of religious faith from involvement in politics and government would be the farthest thing from what the Founding Fathers had in mind.

George Washington, in his farewell address, stated: "Of all the dispositions and habits which have led to political prosperity, religion and morals are indispensable supports. Let us with caution indulge the supposition that morality can be maintained without religion. Whatever may be conceded to the influence of refined education on minds of peculiar stature, both reason and experience forbid us to expect that national morality can prevail in exclusion of religious principle."

People for the American Way—
Fresh Air for American Politics
by Charles V. Bergstrom

Dr. Charles V. Bergstrom, executive director of the Office for Governmental Affairs, Lutheran Council in the USA, is a prominent speaker for the People for the American Way, an organization formed by Norman Lear and others to counter the positions advocated by the new Christian Right. A Lutheran pastor, Bergstrom contends that Moral Majority and other right-wing movements have confused the legitimate advocacy for social justice with the improper attempt to legislate a single morality in a democratic, pluralistic society. The self-righteousness of the right-wing political activists makes discussion of issues very difficult because proponents of the new Christian activism easily assert that they speak for God. In a Niebuhrian vein, Bergstrom cautions that such self-righteousness is dangerous. "There is no single Christian answer to any piece of federal legislation," he argues.

I

Simplistic and unrealistic descriptions of the church's relationship with government are inadequate for these times. In our pluralistic society, hazy ideas of a nation under a Protestant majority are a nostalgic colonial myth. On the other hand, many Christians speak vaguely of a great divide which completely and irrevocably separates church and state. To be sure, the two are institutionally separated in the United States; however, the functions of each bring them together in dynamic experiences of reality. "Absolute separation" is not descriptive of this reality. Increased contact between the church and branches of the federal government necessitates a clear understanding of church-state relations and more concise statements of theology and law which undergird the church's program and clearly state the regulatory rights of the federal government.

Most churches do not envision any great anti-church plot, but there has been evidence of increased attempts by federal agencies to regulate the activities of churches in ways which at times seem threatening to their freedom and to the fulfillment of their ministries. This is all complicated in these years of new approaches to government by some of the right-wing fundamentalist religious groups, those which for many years refrained from any such activity and have in fact made severe judgments against those religious organizations which carried out work specifically related to the government.

Approximately 350 people representing over 90 percent of the mainline and a number of the less conventional religious groups in the United States gathered at the 4-H Center in Chevy Chase, Maryland, early in February 1981. This conference was not a knee-jerk reaction to some specific action or pieces of legislation. Neither did it represent one basic view or approach to government. Rather its reality and its tone went beyond panic or desperation about government actions vis-à-vis the church, beyond efforts to fight big government. It was in fact an effort to analyze carefully and calmly just what has been happening, listen to proposals, and let individual church bodies decide what to do in the future.

The government has a right to regulate in those areas where the fundamental health or safety of society is at stake. It must also

127

be recognized that at times religious groups as such, or leaders of religious institutions, can misuse or break laws. What we see then is a rather interesting gray area. That is what can be best described as the difference between the church's claimed right to define and carry out its mission and its ministry, versus the right of government to regulate in certain areas. There is then a tension, often a creative tension, in determining the proper boundaries of church-government interaction while still affirming the institutional separation of the two entities. Planners and preparers of our Constitution looked far into the future in spelling out the importance of this kind of relationship in our nation.

The differences in approach to the government between religious organizations are not determined by their size, the number of members they may have, their particular hierarchical organization, or indeed any of the outside descriptions that can be given to any of them as religious. They find in their shared concerns the reality of the relationship with government as each of them seeks to carry out their preaching, teaching, and service ministry. There is regularly close cooperation and assistance between those religious organizations (Christian and others) that have in fact tremendously different theological approaches to their faith in God and to their worship experiences. For instance, the Worldwide Church of God with its headquarters in California, has no working relationship with what are often known as the "mainline" church groups. In 1979, acting on the complaint of a few dissident members of the Worldwide Church of God, the California attorney general placed the church in receivership and seized its assets, basing that action on the assumption that churches, as tax-exempt organizations, are public trusts and ultimately owned by the public. A wide variety of mainline religious groups, including the Lutheran Church in America, the National Council of Churches, the California Diocese of the Roman Catholic Church, and the Joint Baptist Committee, strongly protested this action in "Friend of the Court" briefs. Although the U.S. Supreme Court declined to review that particular case, the California legislature stepped in and limited the attorney general's activity in this area.

This points out that religion in America needs freedom, and that freedom ofttimes involves risks. If religious freedom is to be meaningful, the government must operate on the presupposition that the church works for the common good rather than subverting public morals or defrauding citizens. Allowing the government to define narrowly the church and its ministry to get at abuses could lead eventually to unconstitutional establishment of religion, giving force to the religious persecutions of those in office. It is difficult to see how this would really help to overcome the fraud which is often used by the government as the reason for intervention and efforts to force disclosure.

II

In these early years of the so-called new 1980s, there is a different situation that has come about that divides religions and that separates these groups in their approach to the federal government. I have stated clearly that we believe the church has a ministry to fulfill. We believe the church has a right to speak to government. That fact is completely separated from being tax-exempt. This includes, of course, the right of all groups to speak to the government on issues. It includes also the right of government to regulate right-wing fundamentalists as well as so-called left-wing activists. Sometimes those who say "Lord, Lord" do not always speak a good biblical theology. It needs to be recognized that one of the complications is that even those who take the name of God in their presentations can learn to tell false stories about their goals and their activities. Therefore, we need to be aware of all religious groups and their approach to the government in terms of basic theology as far as the churches are concerned.

All of us are aware of the growth in number of the so-called "electronic preachers." Some of these television religious enter-tainers have regular weekly programs and large listening audi-ences. Generally fundamentalist in approach, they have focused these recent years on so-called "moral" problems of the nation as they have defined them. They have defined some of these as school prayer, abortion, defense spending, and homosexuality. Increasingly, their solutions to these moral dilemmas have taken the form of right-wing political positions. This means that they are not only preaching a doctrine to their people and seeking to bring them into the teachings of their religious faith, but they also have approached government in a spirit of evangelism. They have mixed uncritically their ideas of salvation with political decision-making processes.

Now for many years some of us have listened to these revival preachers who said rather clearly that they were conservatives, that they were the evangelicals, that they were those who truly believed in the inspired Scriptures. With Bibles clutched in hand, they would appeal to people to send them their money so that a particular program might be continued and that more people, in their words, might be saved. For a number of years they rejected any participation in political activity, as we have noted. They called themselves the "born-again Christians." (There is of course no other kind of a Christian except one that is born again.) They developed a theory and began to work out their feeling that God has given to them, in the words of Jerry Falwell, "a divine mandate to speak to government." Now this divine mandate has that faulty theological mix of salvation, of saving people, folded into the kind of political view of those who are lobbying the federal government.

Such a mixture is repudiated by mainline Christians and Jewish religious organizations. There is a right and a challenge to speak, but these mainline established religious organizations speak to the government on the basis of advocacy for social justice. They speak to specific pieces of legislation and government regulation. They make no judgments about the individual member of Congress concerning his or her relationship to God. This does not mean that they are less holy or less important. It simply means that they are talking about something different from the gospel of salvation. Most members of the federal government understand this quite clearly, and in Washington, D.C., some thirty-eight religious bodies share meetings twice a month, establish task forces, agree and differ on specific issues, and speak and work together on those that they can. All of this is done in the name of the corporate religious body without any claim that it is God's voice, that it is the Christian or specific individual Jewish voice. Rather it is a ministry of indicating the democratic corporate action. These are the convention votes, the decisions of the church pertaining to issues involving government activity.

But from the right-wing fundamentalists, we have a switch to preaching that this is a "Christian" nation. In fact, one broadcaster has prepared a "*Christian* Bill of Rights." Large numbers of fundamentalists, well over 150,000, marched into Washington in April 1980 in what was called a "Washington for Jesus" rally. Not only was it a religious rally in the political confines of Washington Mall, but a smaller segment of that group received a special mailing encouraging them to be involved in lobbying. That's a bit deceptive. It needs to be pointed out that these television and radio preachers are not the church, that they represent no religious body. They are independent preachers. I am making no judgment here about their relationship with God. We are talking about the church, the corporate church, as we know it in this nation. So they gather in various coalitions; they form and regroup; and very often they do this on the basis of a new issue or a new activity. They jump from a religious rally in Washington to a series of services and programs across the country; to involvement in what they feel ought to be true in terms of the teaching of evolution in public schools, what books ought to be in libraries, and what indeed ought to be seen on public television. There is in all of this that strange mixture of what is often called "morality." Moral Majority is the name of one specific group.

In all of this activity, the change has been made from the church speaking corporately to the government on issues to individual television preachers applying a Christian answer to a political decision. There is no single Christian answer to any piece of federal legislation. These religiously-named coalitions make judgments about the character of individuals. Hit lists are established to get rid of members of Congress who do not vote according to the moral ideas of those who made the lists. Former President Carter was criticized for the "liberal" appointments that he made, and for so-called softness regarding homosexuals. President Reagan was supported and has been called God's answer to their prayers, even though he was divorced. I make no judgment about either man, but point out that they find fault in those whom they want to oppose.

The strength of the religious right-wing fundamentalist movement today is seen not in the power that it may have with organized government. It is seen rather with the illusion of strength which it wants to give and which it is very difficult to truly measure. Recent television ratings and studies by William Martin of Rice University and Jeffrey Hadden of Virginia show that electronic preachers have grossly exaggerated their audiences. We are not members of a Christian republic, and Jewish leaders have every right to express concern about such terminology and about any such descriptions. Although Jerry Falwell will make public his claim that he does not want the cross to be draped with the flag, very often that very picture is depicted on programs and publications of the Moral Majority which is called a political organization.

Many biblical and evangelical Christians find tremendous problems with the theology of some of these individual television religious entertainers. The United States is depicted as God's chosen people replacing the nation of Israel. American history is described in glowing and highly selective terms as they remind us of the good old days of morality. Wealth and success are the expected rewards for good people. A moral America will be powerful again. But the United States is *not* God's people. God's people are scattered throughout the world. The "good old days" included slavery. Wealth and success often were far from God's greatest saints, and a powerful America is not the result of God's reward for some kind of righteousness. Therefore black and other minority groups have every right to be concerned about this kind of emphasis that is worked into church-government relationships, most especially when such preachers are silent about the basic issues of poverty and the need for justice. To be sure, they will occasionally refer to these issues so they cannot be accused of ignoring them. But they have never been a part of their specific and principal preaching programs.

There are obviously some genuine and fine evangelical people in the country who disagree with this new electronic approach to government. Senator Mark Hatfield writes that the

131

grievous sins of our society are militarism and materialism, not opposition to the Taiwan treaty or the Equal Rights Amendment. Evangelical Southern Baptist Bill Moyers has said in one of his programs, "They are being misled, these people, by manipulators of politics masquerading as messengers of heaven. The same Jerry Falwell who claims a divine mandate to go into the halls of Congress and fight for laws that would save America is caught lying in public about a meeting he had with President Carter. Some majority! Some morality!"

Now the strength of these religious right-wing organizations is seen more clearly in their coalitions with secular ultra-conservative lobbying organizations. These are probably well enough known because they use the kind of words that have become important to some these days, words such as "success," "winning," "attacking," "targeting," and "intimidating." Specifically, Paul Weyrich heads the Committee for the Survival of a Free Congress. He was the one who appeared on television the night after the election in November 1980, warning Vice President Bush about his need to become conservative. John T. "Terry" Dolan heads the National Conservative Political Action Committee, best known for its hit listing and for its new programs for future elections. The third name to remember is Richard Viguerie, the editor and publisher of *Conservative Digest*. He is the fund-raiser for the right-wing fundamentalist conservative movements. These are not religious organizations. They are secular lobbying offices. But they use the terms. They talk about morality, and they give the impression of being God's chosen messengers. They are active and they are related. Republican National Chairman Richard Richards has criticized these hit listings.

Three Lutheran bishops issued a statement explaining their deep concerns about the right-wing fundamentalist religious preachers and their mixing together the ideas of salvation and of social justice, their confusing of the issues between church and government. They pointed out that mainline church groups appear before Congressional committees to present evidence and action of the churches, not as the *only* moral choice, but as spokesmen for one decision which has been arrived at by the democratic process of conventions and voting. The Lutheran bishops said clearly:

> We support pluralism and the freedom of all people in the political process in the United States. We maintain that pushing for total agreement on moral issues is not the same as advocating for legislation which will enhance the common good. We strongly discourage members of the Lutheran churches from joining or supporting movements which

confuse church-government relations and distort the church's advocacy mission in the political world.

Again, not only government but also many people of the secular world are able to understand and recognize the difference between trying to convert an individual and trying to state a corporate religious position. We need a patient, persistent ministry of advocacy on behalf of justice, especially for the poor and the oppressed, now more than ever. That kind of activity carries more power than any that may glitter self-righteously under the glare of television lights or appear to be a technicolor flea market in offering all kinds of articles for sale, ofttimes cheapening religious faith in the process.

The present administration seems closely related both to the conservative lobbying organizations such as NCPAC and some of the religious television people. There are also indications of continued support which President Reagan shared at a rally of the right-wing fundamentalists in Dallas in August 1980.

You can be assured that public libraries and public television will be targeted by some of these organizations. We need to be very sure that one religious viewpoint is not pressed on a pluralistic community. You will note also that legislation in the Congress seeks to remove from the Supreme Court of the United States its jurisdiction over specific issues such as prayer in the public schools and abortion. Sensitive areas would then become the decision prerogatives of state governments. All in all, there is a strong effort to establish religion, to recognize the mixture of religious groups and their approach to the federal government. It is truly important that people have a relationship with God. It is just as important that religious organizations work in God's good world for social justice and that people do it with the varied answers and decisions of those who may disagree.

Recently much has been written about modified voices and the changed spirit of the fundamentalist preachers. But they still call those who disagree with them the "liberals," "humanists," and "secularists." Also, much clarifying is still needed about tolerance and respect.

III

In an effort to promote such an atmosphere of tolerance and mutual respect, many, many individuals and numerous organizations are beginning to develop programs of publicity and communication to talk about the necessity for people not only to be involved in political activity, but also to learn to disagree agreeably with one another. The messages that have so often been heard on religious television in recent years about God's judgment and about the moral problems in America may indeed be subjects for presentation. But what we have in this country now is a kind of overbearing threat that intimidates some who disagree. To repeat, it is not the political activism of the right-wing that is criticized here. That is indeed consistent with the American way, but it is the form and spirit of that political action that challenges groups of Americans and has encouraged counter-activities. Not all of God's purity, not all of America's strength can be found in the literal Biblical quotations of one segment of the religious right. There is a problem in the refusal of many right-wing fundamentalists to respect the faith and patriotism of many who disagree with them.

I serve on the advisory board of "People for the American Way." It is made up of people from across the whole political and religious spectrum. They are united in their concern and in their desire to restore confidence in the democratic process, and to encourage citizens to participate. It is not liberals against conservatives in the minds of People for the American Way. They may or may not be religious liberals. Many of these people involved in People for the American Way are deeply convinced evangelicals. Note former Senator Harold Hughes. As a Lutheran, I am a born-again evangelical Christian, confident of God's work through those advocating justice. That is not really the issue. The issue is our concern for justice and that the church's involvement in this concern be just and understanding.

People for the American Way come from all walks of life. They are striving to lead people out of self-doubt and fear that has been instilled; they seek to engender confidence through community participation, mobilizing civic awareness, and fostering understanding with and among different segments of society. They aim at increasing the level and quality of dialogue among leaders and followers, business and labor, and within government. They want to discuss the stands that the right-wing fundamentalists have taken, not on the basis of what they call "Christian" but rather what indeed is best for the common good in a given situation. It may well be that these latter years of the twentieth century will be times of violence. The voices of stridency and division have been loud, although not always clear, in recent years. There are indeed deep problems of domestic and international tension, worldwide inflation and unemployment, maldistribution of scarce resources, military contests, political instability, urban and rural decay. Dialogue is interrupted if any one side claims to have all the truth. Much effort will need to be expended by groups such as People for the American Way.

It will be in the midst of these tensions and polarizations that the real challenge will be faced in making decisions about public libraries, radio and television programming, the authority of the Supreme Court, and fostering understanding of religious differences. Very much as the Washington Interreligious Staff Council brings together thirty-eight religious offices in Washington to share in a ministry of social advocacy, so does People for the American Way bring together a large group of individuals and a broad network of communication people who share a desire to recognize that the secular world is not evil. It is of God, and of people who believe that the recognition of honest differences can be as important to religious faith as Sunday morning television.

Selected Readings

Albanese, Catherine. *America: Religion and Religions.* Belmont, California: Wadsworth Publishing Co., 1981.

Bell, Daniel, ed. *The Radical Right.* Garden City, New York: Doubleday, 1963.

Conway, Flo, and Siegelman, Jim. *Holy Terror: The Fundamentalist War on America's Freedoms in Religion, Politics, and Our Private Lives.* Garden City, New York: Doubleday, 1982.

Falwell, Jerry. *Listen, America!* Garden City, New York: Doubleday, 1980.

Gallup, George, Jr., and Poling, David. *The Search for America's Faith.* Nashville: Abingdon, 1980.

Hadden, Jeffrey, and Swann, Charles E. *Prime-time Preachers: The Rising Power of Televangelism.* Reading, Massachusetts: Addison-Wesley, 1981.

Hofstadter, Richard. *The Paranoid Style in American Politics.* New York: Alfred A. Knopf, 1965.

Jorstad, Erling T. *The Politics of Doomsday: Fundamentalists of the Far Right.* Nashville: Abingdon, 1970.

_____. *The Politics of Moralism: The New Christian Right in America.* Minneapolis: Augsburg Publishing House, 1981.

Kelley, Dean M. *The Uneasy Boundary: Church and State.* Philadelphia: American Academy of Political and Social Science, 1979.

_____. *Why Conservative Churches are Growing: A Study in Sociology of Religion.* New York: Harper and Row, 1977.

Lipset, Seymour Martin, and Rabb, Earl. *The Politics of Unreason: Right-wing Extremism in America, 1790-1970.* New York: Harper and Row, 1970.

Little, David, and Twiss, Sumner B. *Comparative Religious Ethics.* New York: Harper and Row, 1978.

Maidens, Melinda, ed. *Religion , Morality, and "the New Right."* New York: Facts on File, Inc., 1982.

Marty, Martin. *The Public Church.* New York: Crossroads Publishing Co., 1981.

Mead, Sidney. *The Lively Experiment: The Shaping of Christianity.* New York: Harper and Row, 1963.

Morgan, Edmund S. *Roger Williams: The Church and the State.* New York: Harcourt, Brace, and World, Inc., 1967.

Pfeffer, Leo. *God, Caesar and the Constitution: The Church as Referee of Church-State Confrontation.* Boston: Beacon Press, 1975.

Pierard, Richard V., and Linder, Robert D. *Twilight of the Saints: Biblical Christianity and Civil Religion in America.* Downers Grove, Illinois: Inter-Varsity Press, 1978.

_____. *The Unequal Yoke: Evangelical Christianity and Political Conservatism.* New York: J. B. Lippincott Co., 1970.

Rice, Charles E. *Beyond Abortion: The Theory and Practice of the Secular State.* Chicago: Franciscan Herald Press, 1979.

_____. *The Supreme Court and Public Prayer.* New York: Fordham University Press, 1964.

Robison, James, and Cox, Jim. *Save America to Save the World.* Wheaton, Illinois: Tynsdale House, 1980.

Stokes, Anson P. *Church and State in the United Sates.* 3 vols. New York: Harper and Brothers, 1950.

Wilson, John F. *Public Religion in American Culture.* Philadelphia: Temple University Press, 1979.